Additional Praise for *Prepared*

"In *Prepared*, Diane makes a powerful argument that success shouldn't be reserved for a lucky few. She clearly shows how all children can be successful, providing useful insights for how parents and schools can foster self-direction, collaboration, and reflection—the skills our children need to find purpose and fulfillment in their lives. I truly believe this is required reading for any parent or educator who is committed to developing self-sufficient children who can thrive as adults." —ANGELA COBB, CEO of FirstGen Partners

"*Prepared* is for parents and students who are fed up with the high-stakes college admissions arms race. This book brilliantly shows how all kids can succeed in college, find a meaningful career, and live a fulfilled life."
—SCOTT BARRY KAUFMAN, psychologist at Columbia University and author of *Ungifted: Intelligence Redefined*

"Diane Tavenner's courageous book, *Prepared*, is an intimate portrait of Summit schools—their leaders, teachers, and children—putting into practice the science of learning and human development where environments and relationships drive the development of the brain. It is a roadmap by a passionate leader for anyone who sees the purpose of schooling as unleashing the potential of each and every child."
—PAMELA CANTOR, MD, founder of Turnaround for Children and partner of Science of Learning and Development Initiative

"*Prepared* is a roadmap for teachers, principals, parents, and even students that paves the way for every child to reach adulthood and to thrive. Interweaving personal and professional anecdotes of how students navigate the terrain, Diane offers a new and engaging version of high school that prepares every child for college and for a fulfilled life."

—PRISCILLA WOHLSTETTER, Distinguished Research Professor, Teachers College, Columbia University

"*Prepared* is the conversation we should be having as a nation. In this book, Diane Tavenner shows us how authentic, real-world learning and the essential skills of self-direction, collaboration, and reflection can be nurtured both inside and outside of the classroom, giving all parents a valuable guide for helping their children to successfully take on life's challenges." —LINDA DARLING-HAMMOND, Professor Emeritus, Stanford University, and president of the Learning Policy Institute

"*Prepared* tackles the question so many of us parents and educators are grappling with—how do we grow and develop our children and young people so that they can shape a better future for themselves, and for all of us? This immensely readable book pulls us along through Diane's story as a student, parent, and educator who has built some of the most acclaimed schools in the world. It serves as a powerful resource for all of us."

—WENDY KOPP, cofounder and CEO of Teach For All

"This is a compelling and spot-on book from one of the field's most innovative experts. Tavenner won't rest until schools (and society) give young people what they need to thrive, and after reading this book you won't be able to either."

—DAVID YEAGER, associate professor of psychology at the University of Texas

"Getting students ready for a resilient, fulfilled, and happy life requires educators to think about more than just test scores—it requires a fundamental shift in how we think about a school's role in preparing students for success. With over fifteen years at the helm of one of the most innovative school networks in the country, Diane Tavenner knows how to help schools, teachers, and families make this shift, and I'm thrilled that she's sharing her blueprint in *Prepared*."

—MARC STERNBERG, K–12 education program director of the Walton Family Foundation

PREPARED

PREPARED

What Kids Need for a Fulfilled Life

DIANE TAVENNER

CURRENCY

NEW YORK

Currency books are available at special discounts for bulk purchases for sales
promotions or corporate use. Special editions, including personalized covers,
excerpts of existing books, or books with corporate logos, can be created in
large quantities for special needs. For more information, contact Premium
Sales at (212) 572-2232 or e-mail specialmarkets@penguinrandomhouse.com.

LIBRARY OF CONGRESS CATALOGING-IN-PUBLICATION DATA
Names: Tavenner, Diane, author.
Title: Prepared : what our kids need for a
fulfilled life / Diane Tavenner.
Description: First edition. | New York : Currency, [2019] |
Includes bibliographical references and index.
Identifiers: LCCN 2019010643 | ISBN 9781984826060 |
ISBN 9781984826077 (ebook)
Subjects: LCSH: Individualized instruction—United States. | Education,
Secondary—Curricula—United States. | Mentoring in education—
United States. | Group work in education—United States.
Classification: LCC LB1031.T38 2019 | DDC 371.39/4—dc23
LC record available at https://lccn.loc.gov/2019010643

ISBN 978-1-9848-2606-0
Ebook ISBN 978-1-9848-2607-7

Printed in the United States of America

Book design by Jo Anne Metsch

5 7 9 10 8 6

First Edition

FOR ALL KIDS

Contents

PART III: WHAT IS PREPARED?

Author's Note

The stories in this book are all true. I have been fortunate to meet and work with a great number of dedicated educators and inspiring kids. To protect their privacy, I have, in most cases, altered names or certain identifying details.

PREPARED

Prologue

sabella arrived one morning at the start of Summit's second year. She was petite, with perfectly straight dark brown hair, and deep, penetrating brown eyes. She was dressed modestly and carried a school backpack. I didn't recognize her, so I asked if I could help her, and she politely asked to speak with the principal about transferring. "That's me," I said.

We sat down together and the first thing I noticed was her composure and maturity. I was struck that she was a sophomore in high school. Her voice was steady and firm, if quiet. She spoke intentionally and in a measured way, but there was an urgency and resoluteness underneath.

"I want to go to college," she began. "I've heard this

school is different and that you guarantee everyone will be ready for college."

"That's true," I said, and held her gaze. That is Summit's promise. She didn't look away.

"I need a school like this. I won't make it to college if I stay at my current school. In the past, I've been involved in things. . . ." She paused and looked down at her hands before once again meeting my gaze. "With gangs. And with people who don't want the future I want. I'm out of those things now, but at my current school those people from my old life are all around me, pulling me back every day. I don't want to go backward. I want to go forward. I want to go to college."

I felt myself tense up. I did not want gangs at Summit. And, sadly, I'd never met a student who had been able to escape them no matter how hard they had tried. The faces of kids from the previous schools I had worked at flashed through my mind. They all had sincere intentions, but in the end they were unable to change their trajectory, to escape a gang's gravitational pull. I was skeptical that Isabella could. But I was having a hard time reconciling my experience with the young woman sitting in front of me. There was something about her, a steel to her resolve that made me want to believe she would do it.

I handed her an enrollment package and said that if she wanted to come to Summit, she needed to complete it and return it to me. She eagerly accepted it and began thumbing through the pages as I explained the process. It was pretty simple. We asked for standard information and would need a transcript from her current school. She nodded as she followed along, agreeing to complete the forms that evening and return the next day.

As she walked out the door, I made myself a bet that she wouldn't return. I'd met too many kids who wanted a different pathway and would ask for help, only to fail to follow through.

I gladly lost the bet with myself the next morning when Isabella walked through the door. She had meticulously completed all of the forms and ordered the transcript from her school. It would take another day to get the transcript, but she wanted to get what she could to me right away. I flipped through the pages and got to the parent/guardian signature line. It was blank.

I turned to Isabella and pointed out she needed a parent or guardian signature. She looked at me with a determination I would come to know well and said, "I live with my grandmother. She gives me a place to stay. My parents are lost to drugs. I take care of myself."

I nodded. "I understand, but then your grandmother needs to sign the form."

Isabella returned every day that week until at last she had delivered everything required to enroll in high school. Each morning, I found myself hoping she would come back. And so, when I finally told her that she was ready to begin at Summit, I think my smile was as broad as hers. "You won't regret this," she promised.

Isabella turned out to be an excellent student. Her work was meticulous, her thinking clear, her writing advanced, her oral contributions compelling. She was equally strong in math and science and quickly became a peer to another student, Jamie. By all his teachers' accounts, Jamie was gifted. Curious and hardworking, he excelled in all subjects in a way that made it seem as if learning just came naturally to him. He was a well-liked and respected member of the class, giving of his time and always willing to help others. Years later and a few days before graduation, Jamie would share how deeply he admired Isabella. He relished her as an intellectual peer, someone whom he sought out to help him think through arguments and to give feedback on his papers. What he so insightfully recognized was that *he* was not *her* peer in so many other ways. Jamie realized how fortunate he was to live with two loving parents, in a nice, upper-middle-class home, filled with love, food, books, and support. Jamie didn't have to worry about taking care of himself. His job was to go to school, to learn, and to do well. Isabella's life was much harder.

From the time Isabella entered Summit she had always worked at a local retail store near the school. But while in eleventh grade she came to ask if I had any ideas for where she could get a full-time job. Her grandmother's home was a makeshift boardinghouse, and she expected Isabella to pay rent. Isabella also needed to buy her own food, clothes, and supplies.

I offered to help with the food and supplies, but Isabella didn't want that. She simply wanted a job. And so I introduced her to a friend at a start-up technology company just down the street. The company was struggling to hire for a marketing position because it required a fluent Spanish speaker. They agreed to interview Isabella. I wanted to do more for her, but she did everything for herself. Give her a seat in the school and she will make the most of it. Introduce her to a company and she will get the job and excel at it, which is exactly what she did, working every evening after school.

One morning about six months after she started the job, Isabella stopped by my office as she arrived at school. She was carrying two backpacks instead of one. "I'm moving out of my grandmother's house and want to give you my new address."

I knew things weren't good, but this seemed abrupt. I was worried. "What happened? Where are you going?" I asked.

"I've saved enough to get my own apartment. I can't live at my grandmother's anymore. It isn't safe. I'm paying rent, but I often have to sleep on the floor in her room because she rents my space if she can. People steal my food and my things. I can't sleep. I need to leave."

"How can we help?" I asked, eager to meaningfully support her.

"You don't need to do anything. I have an apartment and I'm moving today."

"Well at least let us help you move," I offered with a bit of desperation.

"It's okay, Ms. Tavenner. This is all I have." She pointed to the second backpack. "Can I leave it here and pick it up after school today?" I nodded, feeling a bit useless and incredibly guilty that everything Isabella owned fit into two backpacks.

"Oh, and Ms. Tavenner, I finally saved enough money to remove my tattoo. I'm starting the process this weekend." She flashed the most joyful smile I'd ever seen from her.

It was the tattoo Isabella had gotten when she joined the

gang she had been in. Like everything in Isabella's life, she had independently done what was needed to get out of her gang. It was a harrowing experience, but one she took in stride. And now she was going to remove her last connection to the past she wanted no part of and embrace the future she was creating for herself.

In her senior year, Isabella was accepted to her first-choice college, Santa Clara University, on a merit scholarship to study business. Four years later she graduated, started her career, and created a loving family. She is now planning to start her own business.

To this day, I am inspired by Isabella. I draw strength from her work ethic and determination. I admire her vision, clarity, and the commitment she made to realizing it, no matter what. I aspire to have her level of independence and confidence.

To me, Isabella embodies what all kids want—to be able to live the life they want to live. To be happy, successful, and true to themselves. Like all kids I know, Isabella wanted an opportunity—not someone to save her.

PART I

WHY
PREPARE

Because Graduation Should Mean More

The first Summit Preparatory Charter High School class graduated on a beautiful, sunny June day in 2007 in Redwood City, California, about a half hour south of San Francisco. This graduation looked nothing like any other school's in the nation. There was no alphabetization of graduates by last name, no valedictorian, no outside speaker, no rushing of kids across the stage while the audience held their applause until the end. Just as we'd approached the school itself over the past four years, we wanted to do graduation differently, and intentionally.

We had a temporary campus that year, situated on a portion of the twenty-two-acre Sequoia High School grounds, and we'd borrowed the campus's Carrington Hall for the ceremony. A historic Spanish-style theater built in the early

1920s, Carrington had traditional orchestra, mezzanine, and balcony seating to accommodate four hundred people, and a grandeur that added a sense of seriousness and importance to the occasion. We were finally living up to the promise I had made to all of these families when they took a chance on the school. One of the things that made Summit unique was that 100 percent of Summit's graduates met four-year-college entrance requirements (the national average was around 40 percent). And 98 percent (all that had applied) were accepted to at least one four-year college.

As the school's principal, I gathered with the eighty graduates a good block away from the auditorium so we could line up and enter the theater without parents and family seeing us beforehand, much like a bride enters a wedding chapel. Every such decision about this day had been carefully thought through.

The graduates walked in with their mentor groups. Every student had a mentor, someone who was also a teacher, as well as a group of fifteen to twenty other students they met with throughout their school career. Our mentors had developed special relationships with the students they coached and supported. Each mentor was someone the students trusted, whom they could talk to, who cared about them and their success, who met with them daily, had eaten meals at their homes with their families, and had been their advocate. Sometimes our mentors worked with their students to clarify their academic goals. But just as often, they helped them sort through a problem at home, or navigate a stressful social dynamic.

Each of the graduates was also accompanied into the auditorium by someone who had been important to their journey in life, like a parent or relative. The mentor's efforts complemented those of the family member; together they committed to supporting the student that day, and into the future.

I stopped to straighten ties, reposition caps, to accept hugs and pose for pictures. Isabella grinned a dimpled smile as she teased, "Ms. Tavenner, are you ever going to stop fussing over us?" I poked back, "I'm going to have to. You're leaving me." My heart constricted at the thought, and I moved on before my emotions began to overflow.

The building was filled to capacity. Every single person rose as one to applaud as we walked down the aisle. I watched the faces of the graduates' parents and tried to imagine how I would feel when Rett, my son, would make this walk with me. Tonight, I spied him in the front row with his father, wildly waving his five-year-old hand to catch my attention.

When at last the deep red, heavy curtain was raised to reveal the entire class up on the stage, the crowd exploded into cheers. The fragile control I'd been maintaining broke and tears began to flow down my cheeks, just as I was called upon to speak. Fortunately, everyone was used to me. "Ms. Tavenner is a crier," the students would explain to the new class each year. "She can't help herself. She loves us."

I kept my remarks brief, because the day wasn't about me. The whole ceremony revolved around seeing each and every individual student—letting them know they were all valued and important. It was part of Summit's mission. Each of the mentors told stories about the students in their group, and then, when each graduate crossed the stage, a projector flashed pictures of him or her first as a child, then as a senior, and an audio recording played of the student sharing a quote they'd chosen to capture their journey.

I *knew* these children, or should I say young adults, and their families. I knew how they thought, how they wrote, how they spoke and performed. I knew what they cared about, as well as their fears, and the habits they had formed and struggled with. I knew their dreams, and what they wanted from life. And though I'd participated in countless graduations before this one, for the first time in my career, I honestly *knew* they were each ready to go to college, to be an adult. As the audience departed the hall they spontaneously formed a human tunnel. When the graduates emerged, they were met with a cheer usually reserved for star athletes. They walked a long, loud, supportive gauntlet. And emerged, *prepared* for life.

As I watched them, marveling at how far they'd come, I recognized just how far I'd come along with them.

When I was in third grade, in the late 1970s, my teacher asked me to step out of class with her one day. She was a beautiful, young, popular teacher. She had blond feathered hair, held back in tortoiseshell combs, and wore fashionable bell-bottom jeans and tall wedge heels. She loved butterflies, which adorned her classroom, and most of the girls wanted to be just like her. In my memory, she towered above me, arms crossed, leaning against a cabinet just outside the classroom entrance. I stood before her with my head down, eyes on the ground, feeling exposed and nervous.

She spoke calmly and slowly. "Diane, I'm talking with you today because you are not paying attention. You aren't doing your work." She paused for a moment and I felt her stare boring into me. I braced for what was to come next. She took a deep breath and continued, "And you aren't clean. If you don't change your behavior, your future is not going to be very bright."

What my teacher didn't know as she spoke those words, delivered perhaps to motivate me or at least to scare me into action, was that there had been another fight at home earlier in the week. This one was particularly bad. My mom had been hurt, and the police had taken my dad away. This time he hadn't returned the next morning. I was afraid. And I didn't know what would happen when my dad finally came home. I didn't want to be caught off guard. I wasn't sleeping because I was anxious, forcing myself to stay awake. And I wasn't bathing because I didn't want to be caught exposed, unprotected. My teacher was right. I wasn't focused on doing my work. I was dirty because I was terrified. And now I was ashamed.

But I didn't have a voice to respond to her that day. I couldn't tell my story. I couldn't ask for help. I didn't have the words or the power to change my circumstances. And so I went back into the classroom, sat apart from the other students so as to not bother them with my smell, and tried my best to complete a worksheet.

Statistically speaking, I should not be writing this book. Schools aren't constructed to support a student like me. I shouldn't have earned the degrees I did, gotten the jobs I've had, or worked with the people I've been so privileged to work with. I got lucky. I had some key champions during pivotal moments who saw something in me I didn't see in myself. The bad decisions I made, born from bad circumstances, were fortunately not irreparable. I tumbled my way through school and managed to land in college, where I became a psychology major, in order to try to figure out my life and myself. In an effort to earn extra credit in a general education course, I volunteered in a local elementary school. It was there where I first experienced the joy of helping someone learn. It was a feeling I'll never forget. It was so motivating that I took every opportunity to volunteer, often staying up late into the night to prepare lessons for "my students" while my own classwork sat untouched.

I became a teacher because I thought I could make a difference for kids like me. I thought I could know them and their stories. I imagined defending them so they wouldn't have to experience the fear I had felt. More important, I thought I could take my degrees and training and help to change their circumstances, to break the unproductive cycles I'd learned all about and thought I understood.

In my first few years of teaching, I realized how lofty and unrealistic my goals actually were. I simply *couldn't* get to know each student. So many kids came through my high school classroom in fifty-minute intervals that for every student I got to know well outside of class, there were ten that I didn't. And when I did get to know my students and learned of their problems, I couldn't help them in a meaningful way. What's more—they didn't necessarily even *want* me to. What they wanted was a voice and the ability to help themselves, just as I had wanted for myself.

Those early teaching years were frustrating—heartbreaking, even. I worked with kids to barely get their diploma. In the moment it felt like a huge achievement, but of course "barely" isn't good enough to get into college, or to get a job. I encountered kids who I knew would not graduate at all, and what lay ahead for them was, to me, all too clear. Kids who drop out of high school are less likely to find jobs, less likely to earn a living wage, and more likely to be poor. They're more likely to rely on public assistance, and more likely to suffer from health problems.[1] I knew this, and I didn't see a way I could do anything meaningful to help. I was disillusioned. And it wasn't just the impoverished kids who struggled. I worked in a summer reading program and encountered affluent kids who fell through the many wide cracks in the traditional teaching model. I met hyperdriven kids who it was clear to me had no interest in actually learning the material and just wanted the grade. I saw high school seniors about to leave home who I knew would flounder because they were so dependent on the adults in their lives that they couldn't stand on their own. It seemed we were losing kids left and right. Why couldn't we figure out how to get them ready to be adults, to thrive?

There's a lot of finger-pointing when it comes to education. Parents are blamed for sending kids to school who are undisciplined, hungry, tired, depressed, addicted to their phones or worse. Schools are blamed for not holding high standards, not getting all kids to meet them, and not keeping kids safe. The government is blamed for not spending enough on education and causing the societal conditions that lead to poverty and the breakdown of our communities. I'm not writing this book to add to the negativity. In fact, I look at what has been accomplished in America with a sense of awe. I wonder if we are victims of our own success.

For the greater part of our country's history, most Americans lived in poverty. I can tell you from personal experience, anyone who has ever been poor knows no one *wants* to be poor. When you are poor, your entire life is about surviving and trying to get yourself, or at least your kids, out of poverty. Early in the twentieth century, for the first time many Americans were offered a solid value proposition—prepare your child for the industrial economy and pull your family out of poverty. Employers needed skilled workers to fill jobs, and high school–educated workers could get jobs that moved them into the middle class. Everyone won.

One-room schoolhouses led by the most educated member of the town were replaced by a disciplined approach to ensure the basics were covered and students were prepared for factory life. The same subjects were taught the same way and for the same amount of time. Textbooks, a newer invention, were used to standardize knowledge. Bells, inspired by factory life, were meant to keep everyone on schedule, industrial lockers housed all that was personal, tests were given one time and one time only to sort and rank students. Yes, it looked like an assembly line, but most people were graduating to take just that type of job.

The trade-offs were obvious. Conformity trumped individuality. The high-performers and the low-performers on the discrete skills valued in this system didn't get what they needed from high school, because it wasn't really designed for them, but rather for the "majority" in the middle. Acculturation superseded cultural history and family values. The parents' role in all of this was to ensure their child's compliance: go to school, sit down, and shut up—or else. That child might not have been able to bring his whole self to school, but what he was getting in return—a ticket to the middle class—was worth it. They were counting on him to support the family, and perhaps someday even buy a house. That was the dream. It was real and valuable.

Not everyone would make it through high school, and that was okay, too. Even if the middle class was off limits, the farms still needed people to work them. If a high school diploma and a factory job weren't available, another honorable path was. Society needed a system to sort out who should have which job, so "tracking" kids through school wasn't a drawback—it was a win. Those few who were on the more elite track would sometimes go on to college, and ultimately become the managers of those who worked in the factories.

Around the later part of the twentieth century, though, the value proposition changed. We began the shift from an industrial economy to a more global economy. It wasn't enough to get a high school degree and qualify for that factory job, because the economy became more service- and information-based. Employers changed what they wanted in workers. In the 1950s, the top skills employers wanted were: 1) the ability to work rapidly and for long periods of time, 2) memory for details and directions, and 3) arithmetic computation.[2] But according to *Forbes,* the employees of 2020 need: 1) complex problem solving, 2) critical thinking, 3) creativity, 4) people management, 5) coordinating with others, and 6) emotional intelligence. Employers want innovative thinking, independence, initiative.[3] These were not coveted skills in our grandparents' time.

The impact of these economic changes reverberated. The solid American option of living off the land and farming was quickly disappearing, replaced by industrial and high-tech farming and global competition. You *had* to finish high school. What's more, since it became much harder to get a good job with the skills built in high school, it was no longer sufficient to just pass—one had to do well for the chance to go on. And so began the nuclear arms race for college admissions. The highest priority became not to graduate, but to get accepted to a good college. The standard formula required good grades, good test scores, and lots of activities and extracurriculars. Be the same as everyone else, only better.

As the economy changed, we changed, too. Between 1949 and 1969, the real median family income grew by almost 100 percent.[4] For years, kids grew up to do better than their parents. Today it's an expectation. We dream very different dreams today than we did seventy years ago, because we can—and that's something to celebrate. It's nearly impossible to dream of wanting a fulfilling life when you are focused on food, shelter, and clothing. But as soon as people are able to meet their basic needs they start wanting more, dreaming bigger. The factory job and home ownership aren't enough anymore. Now we want work that's meaningful, so we spend our days doing things that matter to us and that we like. We want to live longer, and to be healthier and more active along the way. We want close relationships with people we care about. We want to be a part of communities with people who understand and accept us. We don't want to trade off financial stability—no one wants to take a vow of poverty in order to be fulfilled—but we've come to think we shouldn't have to choose, that we should be able to have both.

Our country was founded on the premise that every American has a fundamental right to life, liberty, and the pursuit of happiness. The nation has yet to live up to that promise for many of its citizens. And, while the work is unevenly distributed, parents and our education system did work together time and again to prepare kids to pursue the life they wanted. But when things changed, we didn't adapt. In my first decade of teaching, I bore witness to the repercussions. Now, even in the "good schools" kids had to be lucky to get accepted into a top college, emerge unscathed, and feel prepared to enter the next phase of their life. For the schools that already weren't working for kids and families, the odds were impossible. It was clear to me that luck was not a smart national strategy. There had to be a better way.

From Summit's beginnings, we didn't want to build something just for our children. We believed in a new version of high school to prepare every child for college and for a fulfilled life. And part of that "good" life was a world they wanted to live in. We envisioned preparing our children to be contributing members of their community, of society. We wanted to answer questions like: What skills does someone need in a rapidly changing economy? How does one prepare for a life that has financial security and meaning? How does a high school student figure out who they are and what they want out of life? What does it mean to engage in work that feels purposeful?

We knew we would first need to build a school that could do all of these things. Whatever we built couldn't be a specialty school—it had to be both unique and totally replicable, and all done on the public dollar. We weren't just designing a school, we were putting a stake in the ground to show what was possible in educating our kids. We were determined to create an environment that looked at the whole student, a school where every individual was known and belonged to a community. We wanted to teach kids not just what they needed to get into college, but what they needed to live a good life.

Just as important, we knew this had to be a partnership between the school and parents. Parents had to believe in the value proposition offered by the school for their child. It wasn't okay if some kids didn't make it. We had to create a school that focused on every single student.

Our approach was often scrappy—we learned to take advantage of free technology expertise that our home in Silicon Valley had to offer. We took notes from entrepreneurs. We worked with academics who study motivation and mindset, many of whom we cold-called or fan-stalked to make sure we were on the right track. We applied what we learned to the real, everyday work of educating students. We figured out how to help students build and practice everyday habits that support a definition of success that includes college but does not stop there. We showed that if you change the way you look at education, you can both prepare kids for admission to college, *and* prepare them for a good life. It is both revelatory and common sense: you actually *don't* have to trade one for the other.

These ideas were great in theory, but my peers thought I was a lunatic. I would go to conferences and gatherings of school leaders in the growing movement of "college for all" and be called The Crazy Lady. After all, you didn't get kids into college by ensuring they had a sense of purpose. There's a tried-and-true formula for getting into college—grades plus entrance exams—and many believed our job was to simply scale it to as many kids as we could. But at some point, my peers became curious; our success at Summit was hard to ignore.

Our schools—we now have eleven in two states—have seen truly remarkable results. Again, *100 percent* of our graduates are eligible for a four-year college, and 98 percent are accepted. Summit grads finish college at double the national average, and that rate is much higher for our minority students. College completion is what got everyone's attention because that is what provides the best opportunity for economic security. But what mattered most to us was *how* we prepared our students for this success: by equipping each of them to live their own, unique, fulfilling life.

Summit's success attracted national attention. We were one of five schools featured in the documentary *Waiting for "Superman,"* and have over the years been recognized by both *Newsweek* and *U.S. News & World Report* in their national best high school rankings. We've attracted the support of the

Chan Zuckerberg Initiative and the Bill & Melinda Gates Foundation. We're often asked, "What's your secret sauce?" I find myself at social events falling into conversations about schools and parenting. Often people are looking for tips and tricks on how to hack the system to give their own child a leg up. I think they assume because of Summit's success, we must have figured out how to beat the college admissions game, or crack the SAT code. When people begin to spell out the problems of their schools and how they spill into their family lives, looking for me to share a silver bullet answer, I start to squirm. Over the years my husband, Scott, has become adept at softening what can sound like tough love advice, or finding creative ways to exit me from these discussions. But on one occasion I was with a handful of my closest girlfriends and he wasn't there to intervene.

The conversation that night had revealed that many of my friends' children were required to complete hours and hours of rote homework. The problems were the same for every student in the classroom. The kids were unmotivated, frustrated, feeling disengaged. Some of them cried, and most of them didn't like school. Even those doing well were bored. And these kids were still in *elementary school*! The moms felt exasperated. On the one hand, they knew their kids had to excel, even at this young age, if they were to have a chance at good colleges. But on the other hand the trade-offs pushed these moms to their limits. They couldn't reconcile that their kids would have to spend their childhood hating school and the work it involved. Furthermore, these parents didn't want to be the enforcers of things they didn't genuinely value, just to stay ahead in the system.

When they turned to me for advice, I couldn't hold back. "I don't know where to begin. Everything is wrong with what you're describing. It just needs to be completely rethought," I said. These moms weren't confused about the size of the problem, though. They had diagnosed and dissected it with expert precision. That's when my friend Julie turned to me with a level of frustration and concern only a mother can have for her child and said, "Well, what am I supposed to do, Diane? I don't know how to start a school for my child, and he can't go to one of your schools. I bought a house in the best district we could afford, I'm spending all my time working with the school and this is what I've got. So what am I supposed to do?"

I was stunned. They weren't looking for me to affirm all that was bad—they were looking for what they could do about it, right now, for their child. I felt embarrassed that I had been so insensitive. And surprised that someone would want to do what we were doing, and felt they *couldn't*. The work to open our schools had been incredibly hard, with roadblocks every step of the way. So many people thought we were crazy, and were happy to tell me that. It didn't occur to me others might not think we were crazy.

I think about what Julie said every day. How many moms are like Julie? How many parents feel the drive to ensure their child's success is filled with trade-offs that simply don't feel right? How many hold their breath, hoping their child will make it? And what is the cost of that anxiety, stress, and worry, on both parents and our kids?

In that moment, the only thing I could think to do was to make it an option for Julie's school to rethink its approach. If her child couldn't attend one of our schools, maybe his school could at least be like one of our schools. We created a program called Summit Learning, in which other schools could have access to the resources, curriculum, and tools we use, for free. Over the past four years nearly four hundred schools in forty states have taken us up on our offer. We've formed a community of over four thousand educators, working together to support nearly eighty thousand students. But that doesn't seem like enough. It feels like we're moving too slowly.

As I write this book, my son, Rett, is sixteen years old. Soon the day I could only imagine when he was an audience member at Summit's first graduation will arrive. I think constantly about what I've done to prepare him for the world he'll enter after graduation, and how Summit has helped me do so. I think of my friends in similar situations who don't yet have a school that is partnering with them to prepare their child for college *and* life. What do they do? How do I answer Julie's question?

This book is the best answer I have right now. The journey we have been on for the last sixteen years has been a quest to design a school that can truly prepare our children, all children, for the life they want to live—to be the best versions of themselves, to be successful in the fullest way possible—so they can live a fulfilled life. A life filled with financial security, purposeful work, strong relationships, meaningful community, and personal health. While what we have learned is directly applicable to how to "do" school, I believe it is also incredibly informative for how to parent.

In 2015, the magazine *Fast Company* named Summit Public Schools one of the most innovative education companies of the year. I find this funny, because first, we aren't a company—we are a network of public schools. And second, we don't think we've really invented anything. What we have done is take everything we collectively know about what it takes to develop whole, healthy human beings in our society today and put it all together in a coherent approach that actually works. I guess if there is any secret sauce to Summit, that is it.

This book is the story of our journey so far. What we've discovered from the world's experts, but, more important, how that translates into everyday actions and choices that lead to our children being successful. It is a story of people who are searching for and finding a way to have it all— financial security, stability, *and* a fulfilled, meaningful life, on their terms. I also share my own journey, as a child, as an educator, and as a parent whose son is navigating his last years of high school. My hope is that through reading this book, you will connect with a community of people who believe in a new, broader definition of success, and you will know how to better prepare to reach it.

There's so much at stake here, whether you are an educator, a parent, or just a concerned citizen. A strong and thriving democracy requires citizens who are well informed and engaged, who understand the weight of their vote and the value of their voice. In all of the partisan and ideological fights about whether America is great, we often lose the thread of what's most important to our society—its people. In all of our concern about what the role of government assistance should be, we forget that when an individual is self-sustaining and fulfilled, they don't need a lot of assistance. We forget that when an individual is able to live a fulfilled life, it's good for the entire community, for our entire society. In all of our hand-wringing and fear about a nation that is spiraling down, we forget to look at what can spiral us up. My hope is that you will use this book as a handbook, as a guide, a road map, to take stock and take action. As a means to remember how much we all have to gain when a graduation ceremony celebrates our young adults, who are, in every sense of the word, *prepared*.

Chapter Two

Because Good Intentions
Aren't Enough

Like many beginning teachers, I was set up to fail.

Hawthorne High School in Los Angeles felt like a prison, with ten-foot iron fences around the gigantic perimeter and a railroad track running through the middle of the campus. The entire place was physically and emotionally unsafe, marked by daily violence and regular chaos. During the five years I taught there, I became so disillusioned I wondered if there was any hope. I was assigned forty students per class in an aging and dirty facility. I taught the entire day without a break due to chronic understaffing. On my first day I was handed one ream of copy paper, a box of No. 2 pencils, and a one-inch three-ring notebook filled with handouts for which there were no directions or explanations. That was it.

Our students were set up to fail, too. They lived in a low-income community where they rarely saw healthy, happy, and financially stable people who looked like them or shared their backgrounds. Hope for a future in college and career was rationed for very few of the four thousand zoned to the school, and so it was no wonder many didn't brave the dangerous walk to campus, and only a fraction ever graduated. And yet, a lot of students and parents still tried every single day. They didn't have any other opportunity, so they had to make the best of this one. They needed jobs and the ability to make money if they were going to have any chance at life, and they didn't know another way.

I chose to teach here because these kids were a lot more like me than it might seem. South Tahoe High School, where I'd gone as a teenager, was far from the large, urban Hawthorne. South Tahoe had only one thousand students and was tucked into a small mountain town. The three wings of the school were separated by a forested landscape, which was picture perfect, but cold and snowy for a good part of the year. The harsh weather and complete dependency on tourism led to a different type of primarily low-income community. For the most part people didn't feel poor, except in contrast to the visiting wealth that came for the skiing. However, the school itself wasn't much safer or more nurturing than Hawthorne. Fights were common, and bullying was just a part of life. I went most days without ever using the bathroom because it was crowded, smoke filled, and felt dangerous. Our lockers were the only place that felt like our own, and even those would get broken into and vandalized. During my junior year an undercover narcotics officer broke open a drug ring. There was only one honors class per grade so participation was capped.

I thought often of South Tahoe High during my time at Hawthorne. As a high school student, I felt the challenges, but I didn't think about them. I was too busy trying to graduate and get out of town and on to a better life. I came to Hawthorne because I resonated with the students. I chose to work at a tough school in a tough neighborhood, because I thought I could help kids who were like me find a way out. I gave everything I had to my students, my classroom, and my dedicated peers. During the week I was up at dawn. I taught my heart out all day, supervised afterschool activities, and spent the evenings planning and grading. On the weekends I took classes and workshops, and later even began teaching them for others. I was constantly searching for a better way to serve my students.

On Friday afternoons, the teachers would gather at a local Mexican restaurant after what was inevitably a long, hard week. Sometimes teachers from other local high schools would join us and I started to notice a pattern emerging in the conversations. It sounded like we worked in a war zone. Our dialogue was peppered with words like "front lines," "battle," and "hand-to-hand combat." I couldn't deny it felt true and even found myself falling into describing administrators as the "enemy." Later, I would catch myself and feel ashamed. It seemed wrong. High school is where we prepare our children to be adults. How could we do that in a war zone? And how could teachers who cared so deeply about kids become so desensitized to the horrible experience they were having each day?

Perhaps the most disturbing thing of all was that the expectations people had for our students seemed to be lowered each week. The conversation went from preparing all kids for college, to hoping they would graduate and get a job, to wishing they could just learn to read and write a simple three-paragraph essay, to finally just praying they would survive.

I got married during my fifth year of teaching and for the first time started thinking about the prospect of my own family and children. Scott was drawn to move back near home and family in Northern California. As we dreamed and planned I said out loud for the first time what I had been thinking for a while: "Maybe when we move I'll try something other than teaching."

Scott looked at me quizzically. "What do you mean? You love teaching. Why would you stop?"

I hesitated. I often hid the details of my day from him. He worried about my safety and had repeatedly seen me come home devastated when one of my students to whom I'd given so much was pregnant or in jail. "I just don't know how long I can keep doing this," I said.

He chose his next words carefully, knowing I was sensitive when people made judgments about my kids. "Why don't you look for a slightly different type of school when we move? A school that's a little more . . . functional. Why don't you give that a try before you leave teaching altogether?"

I nodded, but deep inside I wasn't sure I could do it.

By May, Scott already had a job and had moved to our new home. I was finishing up the school year at Hawthorne and was scheduled to follow him in a month. I still hadn't decided if I was going to teach or not. And then everything changed.

After a particularly demoralizing day, I walked into our apartment as the phone was ringing. It was my mother, saying she had news of my father. I immediately knew something was wrong. She had finally divorced my dad many years earlier, and he'd remarried and moved to New Mexico. I hadn't spoken to him in years. As she talked, I sank to the floor. Her voice was shaky as she told me Laurie was dead. My stepmother, who was five years older than me and a high school dropout, had been killed in a domestic dispute with my father.

Those next few moments are among the most shameful of my life. The first thoughts and feelings that came to me as I tried to take in the news were so raw and so not the person I want to be. I was shocked, but not surprised. I had seen my father's uncontrollable rage too many times. I was relieved. Maybe now people would believe what it had been like for me growing up. I was disgusted that I could even think such a thing. I hung up quickly.

Laurie's life shouldn't have ended up this way. She'd grown up in an upper-middle-class family in Connecticut. She had a beautiful home, two loving parents, and two very successful older siblings. But for some reason, school didn't work her. In the little time I had spent with her, she had not shared much, but said she never felt she belonged at school; she always felt stupid and bored and as if nothing she learned was relevant. Over her parents' protests she dropped out and moved to California to find a more meaningful life. Sadly, she ended up finding my dad before she found herself.

As I walked numbly around the apartment, I wondered, what if Laurie had had a different kind of school or a different teacher? Would things have turned out the same way? I realized then there was no way I could leave my work.

When I accepted a position teaching English at Mountain View High School, in the Bay Area, I was hopeful many of the problems from Hawthorne wouldn't be an issue on this sixteen-hundred-student suburban campus that was economically, ethnically, and racially diverse. What I wanted most was to be an effective teacher, not just for one or two kids, but for all of my students. I needed a school where there was at least a chance it could happen.

The campus was open, with kids coming and going at lunch, making their way through the surrounding neighborhood on foot, on bikes, and in cars. People calmly moved from class to class, and lazed on the grass during breaks. There was plenty of teen angst, a large and impressive marching band, and lots of sports and activities. The "typical" American high school has been represented in film time and time again, and at first blush Mountain View could have been source material for *The Breakfast Club*, *High School Musical*, or *Pretty in Pink*.

Many parts of my job at Mountain View were positive. For starters, I wasn't breaking up fights between classes and the restrooms were clean and functioning. I taught classes of between twenty-five and thirty students and had access to colored paper in the copy room, which felt like an absolute luxury. Unlike Hawthorne, this place was physically safe and so free of the palpable stress that comes with trying to make it through the day unharmed. However, I quickly started to realize that when it came to opportunity for students, the two schools had much in common.

Even at Mountain View, where the school test scores were significantly higher and the academic reputation much stronger, honors and AP classes were still reserved for relatively few. The school brochures claimed 90-plus percent of graduates went on to college, but when I dug a little deeper, I discovered those statistics were based on students self-reporting their plans in the fall of their senior year. The reality was that only about 40 percent of graduates were even completing the coursework required to qualify for admission to a four-year college or university. Most of our students simply weren't prepared for college, even though all of them entered high school wanting to go.

As a teacher I didn't think I had the power to change these things, and it seemed obvious they needed to be changed. They were clearly impacting my students' ability to succeed. It seemed to me the people who ran schools had that power, and so I decided I needed to become one. I enrolled in the Stanford Graduate School of Education, and simultaneously took a vice-principal intern role at Mountain View. I didn't want to get to the place of wanting to quit again, and I also didn't want to become complacent, so I set out to become the best principal I could be.

Everything I learned I tried to implement. But it was much easier to read about imagined and ideal systems, schools, and classrooms in a book than to create them in practice, especially as people stopped seeing me as a teacher. I walked into the faculty room one day and a group of teacher leaders asked me not to keep a desk there any longer. They explained that even though I was still teaching half-time, now that I was part of the administration they didn't want me eavesdropping on their conversations. I was crushed. The teachers whom I had taken this job to serve now saw me as part of the problem, and everything I was trying to do to set them up for success didn't seem either to stick or to matter much.

After my internship year I became a vice principal, and at the close of my first year in that role, our superintendent called a meeting with all of the administrators. I was the youngest and newest of the group and it seemed pretty clear people expected me to listen and not talk. The issue at hand was parent concerns about district-wide changes. The superintendent opened up a discussion about ways we might address these parents. I got caught up in the moment and blurted out, "We could have a town hall meeting and share all the reasons for the changes. Everything we're doing is in the best interest of kids and we have good reasons. Parents probably don't know all of this, so we just need to share it."

The room was silent and all eyes focused on me. Without hesitation, the superintendent looked at me and said, "That is the dumbest idea I've heard." He moved on. The satisfied chuckles and knowing looks from my seasoned peers were unmistakably clear in conveying the message that I had no idea what I was doing. I was embarrassed and angry. Bringing parents in and working with them wasn't a dumb idea. After all, didn't we all want the same thing?

A few days later the superintendent asked me to lunch to apologize. As we sat in the booth of a local sandwich shop he explained it was time for him to retire. He was frustrated and disillusioned, and there wasn't time in his career to take a new path. He said, "If I were young and starting out again now, I would do it differently. The system is broken. It isn't made to help all kids develop the skills and knowledge they need for the future."

He took a bite of his sandwich, chewed thoughtfully, then said, "If I could do it over, I would start from scratch."

Very early one morning the following fall, I headed to work as usual. I typically made the short drive around 6 a.m., because I liked arriving when the campus was quiet and still dark. I could get so much accomplished in those early hours and feel ready for a day that, once it got going, was nonstop. I planned to run an errand on the way in, but I became engrossed in the news. Before I realized it, I was in the school parking lot. I hustled into my office, pulled out a small cassette radio I still had, and plugged it in. As I tuned in, I called Scott, who was just out of the shower. "Turn on the TV. Something bad is happening," I said. Over the next hour, we listened in shock and horror as the twin towers collapsed. It was Tuesday, September 11, 2001.

That night Scott and I huddled on our couch watching the illusion of our safety and security crumble. Like the rest of the country we were trying to process the horrific tragedy unfolding. We were also trying to make sense of what it meant for our family, as I'd ultimately run my errand—a trip to the drugstore—and a home test had just confirmed I was pregnant. We were going to bring our first and only child into

an entirely different world. On what should have been a joy-
ous occasion, I held our puppy and wondered what it would
be like to hold my child and know I couldn't protect him.

America went to war and the weeks of my pregnancy
ticked away. I would click off the evening news and go to bed
wondering what the world would look like the next day. People kept asking me if my nesting instinct had kicked in. The
truth was I had no idea what they were talking about, but I
kind of hoped there might be a magical moment when, like a
mother bird, I would suddenly know exactly what I was supposed to do as a mom and just start doing it. It was clear I
needed to prepare for my child, I just didn't have any idea
where to start when I couldn't even imagine what the future
would bring.

I was only going to be pregnant for nine months and that
seemed to be flying by. Maybe I should focus on figuring out
what I should do in those first days after my child was born.
Or maybe I should just skip ahead and try to figure out the
later years when kids seemed to get screwed up. Everywhere
I turned I got different and conflicting advice. It seemed clear
to me every decision I was now making, down to the food I
ate at each meal, was going to impact my child, but I wasn't
at all clear as to the "right" decisions. One night we had dinner with a few friends who were also pregnant and the complexity and confusion became apparent when an impassioned
argument broke out about if the fish dish on the menu was
safe to eat. I stayed quiet, realizing I didn't know half of what
these other pregnant women did. I wondered how I had become a bad mom before I even was a mom.

I vowed to do better. My work was busier than ever and

on the weekends we tackled nonstop house projects. Nesting, I suppose. I decided I would at least try to be knowledgeable about *something* I knew would matter in my child's life. For obvious reasons, I picked education.

We had really stretched to buy our house in a neighborhood with "good schools." As I started to ask around and dig a little deeper, I learned that to get into the preschool I drove past every day I was going to have to camp out overnight and hope to secure a coveted spot. And the moms in the neighborhood told me if I wanted to make sure my child got the good teachers in elementary school I would need to start volunteering now for the fundraising committee so I would have influence with the principal. There were tips and tricks about getting into the right playgroups and music classes. Everything was whispered and shared secret club–style because there were only so many spots and everyone was vying for them.

I burst into tears over dinner with Scott. At first he thought it was the hormones, which it partly was, but he quickly realized it was more as I unloaded all of the stories and advice I'd been getting.

"It just seems crazy to me," I said. "Every parent wants their child to succeed. I want all of my students to succeed. How is it good for anyone when kids fail? Why do there have to be winners and losers?"

Twenty miles away in Portola Valley, a dad named Chris Buja was having the exact same thought.

chapter Three

Because It's a
Solvable Problem

Chris Buja didn't think about the state of his neighborhood's high schools very often. It was the late 1990s, and he had plenty else on his mind. He and his wife had relocated to Silicon Valley from Washington, D.C., and he worked at Cisco as an engineer while his wife worked at Oracle. The couple had a young son, Spencer, who was just about to start kindergarten.

Chris—an Illinois native with a tall rower's build, reddish hair, and a fair complexion—had become close with their nanny's teenage son, Swain. Swain loved to write and, based on what he'd shown Chris, was pretty good at it. He wanted to attend San Jose State after he graduated from Menlo-Atherton High School in 2000. Chris felt a sense of responsibility for Swain, whose own father had died, and offered to help him with his college applications.

As Chris dug in and helped Swain apply, he realized the high school senior hadn't taken the classes he needed for admission to the California State University school system. When he explained this, Swain shook his head. "That can't be," he said. "Most of my friends aren't graduating. But I *am*—so why can't I go to college?"

"Wait," Chris said, "let's stop there. What do you mean, most of your friends aren't graduating?"

Though Chris had already heard some rumblings about parents not being happy with high school options, it hadn't loomed large on his radar because his son was so young. But he was appalled that Swain—a good kid who was working hard in school—hadn't even realized he wasn't taking the classes he needed to be eligible for a state college. And if what Swain said about his friends was true, the situation was even worse than Chris realized.

Soon after the conversation with Swain, Chris attended a meeting the local paper had called with the community. *The Almanac* wanted to hear what residents cared about that the paper wasn't covering, and a woman stood up and said, "You're not covering the biggest issue, high school. People are leaving this community in large numbers because they're unhappy about the schools." Inspired, Chris placed a meet-up ad in a middle school newsletter to see what might be done about "the high school problem."

Thirty parents showed up, and another thirty or so responded to say they couldn't attend the meeting but were worried. In no time, the group swelled to more than two hundred parents. They were concerned about overcrowding, safety, and boredom, but it was more than that. A majority of parents felt school on the whole was missing the mark, that it wasn't preparing kids for the world they'd enter. They wanted their kids to get into college, of course, but they also wanted them to have good lives. And school didn't seem equipped to teach them the necessary skills.

Chris and the other parents wondered why. Companies were so desperate to find qualified people to fill good-paying jobs, they were lobbying for more visas to be issued for foreign workers. Why couldn't Menlo-Atherton prepare kids from their own community for these roles?

The group of parents who had now formed the Community High School Foundation weighed many options. A public charter school would be the least expensive and the fastest to implement. Even though they hadn't set out to start a school, this was the clear winner.

The Foundation recognized they had no idea how to design or run a school, and so the first step was to find someone who did. They sought advice from the Stanford Graduate School of Education, and one of my former professors put them in touch with me.

We so rarely get to start from a place of wondering what might be possible. As educators, as parents, as human beings, we most often stay within the confines of what is. But in graduate school, my favorite teacher of all time, Larry Cuban, invited me to ask, "What if there were no constraints?" In an assignment for his class that would forever change my thinking, I had to write a paper to answer the following deceptively simple question: "What is a good school?" For years I had been pointing out and trying to fix all of the problems I so clearly saw in the schools where I taught. But never once had I stopped to think, what would these schools look like if they were just good? From a blank piece of paper, I got to design—not fix—a school. The opportunity was exhilarating, the responsibility overwhelming.

The vision I shared with the Foundation came from my "good school" paper, which was grounded in my own experience, and incorporated the science and research I'd learned at Stanford. While we were coming from different experiences, the parents who formed the Foundation and I wanted the same things. We shared a common vision.

When I got the offer to lead the Foundation's school, I wasn't able to contain my excitement and fear. Scott and I had agreed that though I wanted the job more than anything, I wouldn't accept it if the community was uncomfortable with my pregnancy—which they didn't yet know about. I understood why it would give them pause—they were taking a huge chance on me, and they also expected much of me. I didn't know what it meant to be a new mother. What if I couldn't do it?

I met with three Foundation representatives at a Starbucks near my house, and told them I was expecting. I said it would be okay if they wanted to rescind the offer. I deeply respected all of the work so many had done and I didn't want to undermine it. I'll never forget the looks on their faces. At first, a furrowed brow—was it frustration or confusion?—

and then glances among them. Finally Chris said, "It's even better you're pregnant. Now you're a parent. Congratulations and welcome!"

The direction of my life was about to change.

In May 2002, I delivered my first child, Rett. And on July 1, I launched what I have come to consider my second child, Summit Prep. We had just over a year to find a building, design the program and curriculum, hire the faculty, recruit students, and secure start-up funding. It was going to be a race to finish on time.

As I recruited families to our new school, I promised a lot. I started by guaranteeing every single graduate of Summit would be accepted to a four-year college. And every student would be known and known well by a mentor who would work with them and guide them for all four years. I promised all of our students would be equipped with academic skills, and with the real-life skills they would need to be successful and to contribute to society.

My cell number was the only official contact for Summit, and so I fielded calls at all hours from families who wanted to ask me questions or set up a time to meet with me. I quickly realized most parents willing to engage with me had children for whom school really wasn't working. "My child is different," they said, "and I want to know how your school can help."

Ryan's parents told me they worried he would become just a number and get lost in a big school. Ryan was a bright, sensitive kid who had always been an excellent, curious student at his Montessori school. His parents just couldn't imagine sending him to a crowded, tiered high school where he'd be run through what they thought of as a mill. They worried it would squash his spirit—he was a whole human being and they wanted him to be seen that way. I promised there was a place for him at Summit. We would challenge him academically but never lose sight of the fact he was more than just a grade.

Maya's mom's concerns were completely different. Maya was a tiny girl with thick glasses that magnified her already large eyes. Her family was middle-class, and Maya had gone to a fairly good elementary school. She had always struggled in school, and when she was diagnosed as dyslexic, her mom enrolled her in Charles Armstrong, a private school specializing in dyslexia. "Maya is smart and funny, but no one knows what to do with her. I don't think anyone really believes she can be successful," her mom said as Maya looked on knowingly. The family was very open, so nothing her mom said came as a surprise to Maya. "Is there a place for her at your school?"

"Yes," I said. "Absolutely." Every student would have a *Personalized Learning Plan,* or *PLP,* I explained. We would look at what Maya needed and wanted and we would make sure she got it. "You will not have to fight to get her into the right classes," I promised. "We will be able to support her throughout high school." This mom had been through the wringer. She knew she had an amazing kid, but one who struggled. She knew she wanted the best education for her child, and had sent her to Charles Armstrong at great financial cost. And now here I was, telling her, "Don't worry. I will make sure Maya gets into college." It was a promise she accepted with a healthy dose of skepticism and not one I took lightly.

I met with families who looked at the graduation track record of the school their child was set to attend, and knew their kid had no chance to go to college if they took that route. They could take a risk on Summit because they had nothing to lose. One parent I met with in this category was a single mom of two daughters, and her oldest, Jennifer, struggled mightily. Jennifer was extremely heavy, socially awkward, and had some clear cognitive challenges. She pulled a rolling backpack around everywhere with her, and when she got excited, she would pump the handle. Any teacher would have immediately recommended her for testing, but her mother made clear she would have none of it. Unsurprisingly, Jennifer had struggled in school, and every time it got too difficult academically or socially, her mom—who was intensely protective—removed her and enrolled her in a new school. "Don't worry," I said. "I will make sure Jennifer gets into college, but, more important, that she is socially safe."

Miguel's mom worked three jobs and, while too overextended to know much about what public school had to offer her son, she knew it wasn't enough. She herself had little education. Miguel's dad wasn't in the picture. Miguel was quiet—he had a really hard shell and I couldn't pierce it to begin to understand his story. His middle school had been rough—that I knew—and later I would learn he'd been a heavy drug user while a student there. I looked at his mother and told her I would get him into college.

Then there was Eric. He had been diagnosed with leukemia, and no one knew what his future held. The diagnosis had turned the world of his family upside down, and changed what his parents wanted for him out of high school—as well as what he wanted. Eric was an only child, and faced with the real prospect of losing him, his highly educated parents decided they didn't want him to be miserable for the next four years as he fought his way through the Advanced Placement track in his big high school. I promised Eric's parents they didn't have to choose. Eric could get a quality AP education without spending six to eight hours a day doing homework. They didn't have to trade their son's happiness now in order to secure his future success.

In the end, on paper our initial class of eighty freshmen wasn't the group a school would traditionally place in their college track. But unlike at my previous schools, I already knew every single student and family. I had spent countless hours talking with them and so I knew their hopes, dreams, worries, and fears. They were just regular teenagers, each with unique interests, needs, strengths, and challenges. I had looked into their parents' eyes and said, "Trust me. They'll be ready for college and they will be good, happy people." And I believed they could be.

Throughout the planning year, I worked closely with Kimberly, a parent on the Community Foundation Board. Kimberly's three boys were younger, but like many, she was planning ahead for high school and had invested nearly two years of work into bringing the school to life. I talked to Kimberly daily—sometimes multiple times a day. I spent hours at her house working on timelines, plans, and budgets. She had emerged as the leader of the community and understood business and operations, but she wasn't an educator. Much of the time we spent together was in conversation about my plans for the school.

Kimberly was a Stanford business school graduate and seemed particularly concerned with getting her kids accepted to top colleges. I worked hard to help her understand that the best way to get her kids accepted to selective schools was to help them develop their sense of purpose and to really understand who they were as unique individuals. I made the argument that, contrary to her experience, this could be done while developing the skills they needed for college, work, and life. She remained skeptical, and I grew worried she didn't believe in what we were trying to do.

One night Kimberly called me to share a "deep concern" she had been stewing over for several days. She wanted to know exactly how I was planning to make Summit a college prep school when so many of the students I was recruiting were not college prep material. We talked late into the night and for hours and hours over the coming days and weeks. That call was the beginning of the unraveling of our work together.

As we got closer to opening our doors, it was becoming real—and scary—for everyone. At her core, Kimberly didn't believe all students could be prepared for college. She believed students had to have a certain level of preparation and ability in order to be college-bound. If they didn't have it by the time they were in eighth grade, they either didn't have the talent, or the work ethic, to succeed in a college prep school. In Kimberly's mind, we had to find a way to accept only students who had what it would take to be college-bound, or the school would fail.

I was stunned. I felt like I was back in the Mexican restaurant on a Friday afternoon with teachers from Hawthorne High, surrounded by expectations of kids that sank lower with each passing day. But this time, I had *guaranteed* eighty families I would prepare their child for college. I had given my word. The prospect of going back on that felt unacceptable. I don't make promises I can't keep.

At 10 p.m. the night before the first day of school, Kimberly sent an email to me and the board. She said the school was "doomed to fail" because I'd recruited a class of kids who would never be college-ready. They would hold back the kids who could otherwise make it. Implied, though not explicitly stated, was that she would not want her child to go to Summit. How could we serve the needs of her child while dealing with the others?

I felt angry, undermined, and unsupported. I also felt determined. *Don't tell me I can't do something,* I thought. *I will prove you wrong.* The battle lines were drawn for the future of Summit. The stakes had never felt higher and I didn't intend to lose.

I also felt baffled by Kimberly's perspective. Why was it so hard to do something that seemed undeniably good? Why would people and institutions try to block us from treating and preparing every kid in the way their parents would want them to be treated and educated? Why was it okay for Kimberly to expect her own kids would go to college, but not

other people's children? I would encounter many more people over the years who shared Kimberly's mindset and I felt
the same confusion every time.

Luckily, the board felt differently. Kimberly's concerns
prompted six long months of meetings and discussions before the board finally put a stake in the ground and officially
affirmed the design and direction of Summit. Kimberly was
their friend and neighbor. Their children played together and
they socialized on the weekends. It wasn't easy to rupture
these relationships over a school none of their children were
yet attending, in defense of me, a woman they hardly knew,
and for eighty students, many of whom were really struggling in their first semester. The fact that they did gave me
courage and validation I've drawn upon for the last sixteen
years.

Kimberly resigned immediately following the board action. "You can win the battle and lose the war," my mom
often said. As I stood reading Kimberly's resignation letter,
my mom's warning played on a loop in my head.

During our most recent board discussion, one of my board
members had said, "Diane, you have a vision for a school
community that is different, and much better than what we
have today. I can see your vision. It's like a beautiful carriage
and it's perfect and everyone wants to ride in it. But the reality is, the school we actually have is a start-up and right now
it isn't a beautiful carriage at all. It's a rickety wagon that
doesn't look very safe for travel. No matter how beautiful the
picture you paint is, most people aren't going to risk putting
their child in the rickety wagon. So build the beautiful carriage as fast as you can."

We had won the right to build the school we envisioned. Winning the right to align the work I loved with my personal values felt incredible. The opportunity to build a school that valued and supported every child in the way I would value and support my own child was exactly what I'd been searching for. But we hadn't built it yet. I would soon realize the work to get this far, while hard, would pale in comparison to what we would face in the coming months and years. The real work had just begun.

PART II

HOW
TO
PREPARE

I don't know much about the invention of GPS. I just know how much it changed my life for the better. First with a little device I could put in my car, then built into my car, and now on my phone and in my pocket wherever I go, GPS is a game-changing improvement over paper maps.

Growing up in a small town like Lake Tahoe meant that all of the places I was going were familiar. I'd been going there most of my life and if something was new, it was pretty easy to get verbal directions: "Drive a few minutes past the dump and look for the yellow house on the right. Turn left there, then make an immediate right." When I moved to Los Angeles everything changed. Not only did I not know where anything was, but now I was confronted with a gigantic, sprawling city that made absolutely no sense to me. I was late and lost often. I didn't like being late or lost, and I really didn't like it when I would explain to someone how I had arrived at my destination and they would say, "Why didn't you . . . ?" There was always a smarter route if you understood traffic patterns and side streets.

The first time I used GPS it seemed to be a bit of a miracle, and it's improved dramatically since. I still tell it where I'm going, but now it incorporates all types of information about traffic and road conditions to help me figure out the best routes. It also gives me a lot of choice and control. It will share different pathways and show the difference between them, it will adjust to changing conditions, and some GPS apps allow me to contribute information to help everyone using the system. By helping one another we actually each find better pathways to our respective destinations.

The chapters in this section—covering real-world projects, self-direction, reflection through mentorship, and collaboration—are the route Summit uses to prepare kids for adulthood and a fulfilled life. They are our core pillars. While each makes sense on its own, they also build on one another. Real-world projects lose their impact without the skills of self-direction. The self-directed cycle—a process by which students set a goal, make a plan, implement the plan, and then show what they've done—isn't complete without the ability to reflect, with the guidance of a trusted mentor. Collaboration makes each of these possible, and all of the other chapters make true collaboration possible. Used together, they are like the most up-to-date version of GPS, creating the smoothest passage for students to the ultimate destination of the prepared adult.

Chapter Four

Real-World and Project-Based Learning: Speaking Out

I walked out of my office and almost tripped over the orange cones lined up in the hallway, only to have to quickly scurry out of the way so as not to collide with a student. Lailah, a slight ninth-grade girl with hair pulled back in a messy pony-tail, had her eyes trained directly forward. She wove her way through the cones while reciting what sounded like a speech. "For instance," she said, "while many people think they know what's in their food, few people actually do."

From around the corner, the ninth-grade-English teacher, Adam Carter, called, "Lailah, Ms. Tavenner is a real-life ob-stacle. You need to be mindful of her, without losing focus." As I made my way to Adam, wondering what in the world was going on, he issued four loud beeps from a bullhorn and closed a door, putting up a blockade and forcing the students to reroute.

"What are you guys working on?" I asked Adam, after giving him a hard time for calling me an obstacle.

With a sly smile and in his disarming southern drawl, Adam said, "Sorry, Diane. No time to talk right now, but feel free to ask one of the kids. They'd be happy to share." And he was off.

I scanned for an option. Every student seemed to be completely engrossed, so I hated to interrupt. But Adam was intentional—he wouldn't have suggested I talk with a student unless it really was okay.

"Hey, James," I called, gesturing to a tall, slim, studious boy. "Is it okay if I interrupt to ask what you guys are working on?"

"It's fine, Ms. Tavenner. We're practicing staying focused when there are interruptions and obstacles, so talking to you is good for us."

"What are you focusing on, exactly?"

He explained they were working on *Speaking Out,* which Adam had designed with our history teacher, Kelly Garcia. It was a multipart project: First, students had to choose how to use their voices to make a change in their community. What did they think could be different or better? Then they had to really research their topics, to become subject-area experts. The third and final step was to develop and give a persuasive speech to convince other people to change.

"So what's your topic?" I asked.

"I'm trying to convince people they should end farm subsidies."

"Whoa! Why did you pick that?" I wondered with a bit more surprise than I should have shared. Why would a ninth grader in Silicon Valley be interested in farm subsidies? How would he even know about them?

"Well, I started out thinking I really wanted to change taxes. My parents are always complaining about taxes and, I mean, what are we really getting for our taxes? But then when I researched I saw how a ton of tax money is going to pay people not to grow food. I couldn't get it out of my mind and I couldn't believe anyone who really understood it would support it. We could be spending that money on so many more important things and using that land to feed people. So I decided I really had to do something about it."

"How are you going to get your friends to care, though?" I asked. It seemed a reach to me. "And even if they do care, how are you going to convince them to act?"

James gave me a slightly confused look that held a hint of condescension (something you get used to when you work with teenagers). "Ms. Tavenner," he said, "just because we're young doesn't mean we don't care about things. We *really* care when things aren't fair—especially when we have to pay for it. I'm just going to show them how to follow the money and when they find out where it's going, they'll care."

I let James get back to his speech and carefully made my way through orange cones and down the rest of the hallway. Though I went on with my day, James came back to mind when, just a few hours later, I had a completely different conversation with another ninth-grade boy.

This time I sat in the back of a classroom at a local high school. It was hiring season, and I wanted to observe a history teacher in the running for a role at Summit the following year. I'd been in the room for about forty-five minutes and so far I had seen the teacher take attendance, collect the homework, and give a short lecture on the causes of World War II while students took notes. He then walked around the classroom, monitoring students, who read from their textbooks and started to answer a series of questions they would finish as homework.

The class was calm and compliant, and people looking in would say most of the kids were doing their work. But from my angle in a back row, I noticed several students doodling and others passing notes during the lecture. Others seemed to just be zoned out, and one had his head down the entire time. The student I decided to talk to sat in front of me and had spent the bulk of the class period drawing a very elaborate battle scene in his notebook.

I tapped him on the shoulder and whispered, "Hey, I'm a principal from another high school. Do you mind if I ask you a few questions?"

His eyes darted to the teacher, but then he shrugged. "Sure."

"What are you learning today?"

There was that look, like *Are you serious, lady?* "Uh . . . history."

"I'm sorry. Yes, obviously history, but I mean, what specifically are you really learning and why?"

He stared at me a bit blankly and then said, "I have to pass this class to graduate and I need it if I want to go to college."

Sensing I wasn't going to get any more on why it might be

important to learn about WWII, I asked, "What do you think of this class?"

He loosened up a bit. "It's fine. It's normal. Mr. Rogers is pretty cool. I mean, he seems to care and he tries to make it interesting by telling some cool stories sometimes. Sometimes we have discussions and those are okay," he offered.

"One last question and I'll stop bothering you," I said. "How do you feel about school?"

He leaned back and paused for a moment. It seemed he was weighing how honest he wanted to be. "It's pretty boring, but that's school. Everyone hates it, but it's what we all have to do."

PROJECT-BASED LEARNING

I drove back to Summit Prep thinking how starkly different the two conversations were, even though the two boys had a lot in common. For that matter, the experience and training of the teachers was similar. The big difference was the approach to learning. Could this teacher believe another way was possible? Could he let go of his experiences and training enough to learn a different approach? It was the number one thing I weighed in hiring.

Most high schools still follow a mostly traditional approach to learning. Students learn information about a subject through "units" like "The Industrial Revolution" and "The Life Cycle of Plants." Units are made up of lectures, and the students take notes, read textbooks, and respond to questions or solve math problems. The unit might include film clips or presentations with more notes, followed by teacher-led discussions and reviews of the questions, and ultimately a multiple-choice or short-answer final test. Sometimes an essay is assigned. There are quizzes along the way, lots of homework, and students are expected to make flash cards and study. It all sounds familiar because it's how most of us were taught.

Great teachers work hard to make their lectures entertaining and to include small-group work. Science teachers offer labs, and English and history teachers assign papers. Sometimes a teacher will assign a final project, but for the most part, these are the *dessert,* not the main course, and generally only happen a few times a year.

Since our goal at Summit is for kids to develop the skills and habits they need to be successful in life, our learning is designed to be focused on the real world every single day. Well-designed projects are the most effective learning approach to achieving this goal, so this is how we've organized everyday learning. Projects begin with a problem, question, or challenge that is relevant to the student and his community and life. They end with the student performing a task that directly addresses the problem, answers the question, or meets the challenge. As the student moves toward a solution, he gets timely and actionable feedback, so he improves as he goes. It's not that students don't learn about the industrial revolution or life cycles—they do. But they learn about them through a project that makes the connection to their life, and gives them the space to problem-solve. A history project might be "The Industrial Revolution: The Story of a Product," wherein students trace a product from its invention to how it's used today. In building a deep knowledge of the product's journey, they come to understand the larger industrial revolution. A science project might be "The Electric House," where students learn how engineers apply scientific knowledge to make predictions, create accurate designs, and achieve engineering goals. Acting as engineers, students design physical models of buildings and the electrical systems that power them. In the "Dear Editor" project, students are asked to consider how writers and media outlets utilize logic and logical fallacies to convince or distract their audience by actually assuming those roles.

These projects aren't wedged in, but rather are the day-to-day work of the students. Lectures are replaced with deep discussion, planning, research, model making, writing, and lots of critical thinking as student and teacher work side by side. These projects aren't relegated to the wee hours of the night before they're due, and look nothing like a poster board with hastily written paragraphs and home-printed pictures. The final products are high-quality presentations, models, simulations, websites, campaigns, building plans, and businesses. Projects aren't dessert—they're the main course.

I was at Michaels craft store looking for birthday cake supplies when I stumbled upon the California Mission Project kits. They caught my attention because of my extreme distaste for the California Mission Project. As a mom, I had spent one very long weekend searching for every Lego Rett had in a shade of brown so he could construct a mission for his fourth-grade project. The assignment was the epitome of a dessert project. The kids had been given several handouts with a picture of a mission, labeled by part, and a short passage on what it was like to live in a mission. They had "studied" this information and taken a vocabulary and short-answer test about their knowledge. They concluded their study of missions with an assignment to construct a mission and label its parts. They could make their missions out of whatever they wanted, which was billed as student choice. The only redeeming part of the experience for Rett was that he loved Legos and so at least got to build with them. The California state standards require every student in California to study the missions. The mission assignment has become so common that a company saw a business opportunity in it—to manufacture a kit to fulfill the project requirements. Just go to Michaels, buy the kit, and follow the step-by-step instructions for assembly, just like putting together a piece of IKEA furniture. There is no real learning involved. Rather, it just requires a parent who can afford to go buy the kit and help the child to follow the directions or, in many cases, do it for them. While it's important to learn about California history, I found the "project" to not only be a waste of time for kids, but counterproductive, in that it created an expectation in people's minds of what a school project was. A real-world learning project entails something much different. Quality projects can be developed for any age group, and become more advanced with each grade level.

Our seniors participate in a project called Sim City— created by a group of science teachers who were striving to attract their teenage audience with a title straight out of the video game world—that starts with some big questions: How can we design a more sustainable city? What kinds of decisions do people, companies, and governments have to make regarding the use of natural resources, pollution, and waste management? How does the cost-benefit analysis influence these decisions?

Students get to choose if they want to assume the role of a city planner and redesign a real city facing sustainability challenges; or if they want to respond to a contest challenge to design an entirely new city from scratch. For two full months, the students work in teams, and their design must consider agricultural, energy, industrial, and residential tensions. They have to justify their decisions with research and evidence. And they also need to balance personal beliefs, environmental impacts, financial and societal costs, and the beliefs and needs of the city's citizens. What are the trade-offs of their decisions? How do they justify their choices? What complaints are they likely to receive, and how will they defend their plan?

I recently brought a group to observe the students at work on Sim City. The final presentation was just a week away, which students would give in front of several local city planners and a few executives from design companies.

After I explained the project to the visitors, one looked at me with exaggerated skepticism. "I never did anything this hard in *college*. You're trying to tell me all of your high school seniors are doing this?"

I had to admit, Sim City was challenging. Every time I read the project description, I gulped and wondered how well *I* would do. That said, I'd seen this project plenty of times before, and I knew what our seniors were capable of. They had been practicing this type of critical-thinking work every day for four years, and slowly but surely, they had grown and developed so they could take on a project this complex. Not to mention, it felt relevant to them. They were graduating soon, and starting to think about where and how they wanted to live. Urban, rural, or more suburban? What were the repercussions of this choice, as far as their transportation budget, impact on the environment, and culture? The Sim City project allowed them to really dig into what they were naturally grappling with anyway.

I swung the classroom door open and with a welcoming wave of my arm said, "Let's see."

Each group had a model of their city. In some cases it was a physical model that could rival those I'd seen in the windows of architecture firms. In other cases it was computer-generated. Every building, road, structure, and plant had a purpose behind it. I asked questions about item after item and got thoughtful response after response.

"It's a living roof garden that can feed people with hundreds of gallons of water per day. It also doesn't pollute," said Andrea, a girl from one team.

"Wait, what?" a visitor asked. "How does it do that? And what do you mean it doesn't pollute?"

"Because it's an ecosystem. The living things and nonliving things are all part of a system and get used in it; they cycle through each other."

As we spent more time with Andrea's group, I noticed that while she fielded questions about the environmental science, another of her teammates answered questions about demographic issues, and another fielded more-mathematical questions. I asked them to explain why.

"There was a lot to learn," Andrea said, "so we divided up

and became experts in different areas. We would bring every-thing together and then make decisions."

"But how did you decide who became expert at what?" I pressed.

One of her teammates, Michael, explained that they picked what matched their interests and strengths. They didn't shy away from what they needed to get better at, but were intentional about pairing up accordingly. "I'm really good at mathematical modeling," Michael explained, "so I teamed up with Carlos, because it's one of his growth areas. But he's really knowledgeable about genetically modified foods because he did his tenth-grade Passion Project on it." The *Passion Project* is a sophomore tradition at Summit, wherein students get to choose an area to dive into and re-search deeply. "So," Michael continued, "he led on food sources and agriculture."

"We all needed to learn from each other to make good decisions," Andrea said, "so you had to have your area *down*, you know? So you could teach it to everyone else."

"Hey," Michael said suddenly, "can you guys help us pre-pare for our presentation next week? Tell us what questions or objections you have. We need to get ready for pushback from the city planners."

When I finally led my group of visitors out, I knew the first assumption I'd hear, because I heard it all the time. And sure enough, before the door had even shut behind us one of the visitors said, "Those must be your top students. They were amazing."

I explained that every single one of our seniors was doing this project, regardless of what skills or habits they'd come to Summit with. Their ability to perform so well was not happenstance but the product of years of their hard work, and the careful planning and coordination of all their teachers.

I think of what happens at Summit like an inspirational sports movie montage. Sports movies *always* have them. The movie opens with a team that for whatever reason isn't able to win, but has heart, passion, or purpose. At some point, something clicks and then you see the athletes busting their butts over what is really just a couple of minutes but is suggested to be months and months. Just like the coach who stands on the sideline pushing and inspiring the athletes, our teachers create really hard and interesting experiences that simulate the big event. In the same way the athletes work all the muscles they'll need in the movie's climax, our kids work all of the skills and habits they'll need when they leave us.

What happened in that senior class was the result of four years of real-world "workouts," with constant feedback from dedicated coaches, and tons of hard, push-them-to-their-limits practice on issues the kids cared about and were interested in. Those years weren't exactly cinematic or set to music, and they felt long and often messy. But the result was that by their senior year, those kids were in shape for the main event.

PROJECTS AREN'T NEW

Summit is by no means the first school to adopt *Project-Based Learning,* or *PBL.* These kinds of projects go back to the early twentieth century in the United States. A book called *The*

Project Method was published in 1918, and in the 1920s an Illinois superintendent had first graders create a school post office so they could understand how one worked.[1] In formal terms, PBL works as "a teaching method in which students gain knowledge and skills by working for an extended period of time to investigate and respond to an authentic, engaging, and complex question, problem, or challenge." But the vast majority of schools don't do PBL at all, and the relatively small number that do—and even tout their adoption of it—often still use it as a "nice-to-have," like the cherry on top of a sundae. PBL is *not* what most kids are doing every day, day in and day out. But when you consider the evidence in favor of learning this way, it's hard—at least on the surface—to understand why.

Research has shown that when students learn through projects, they retain what they've learned for longer, and they understand it more deeply.[2] The project approach doesn't compromise test scores, either; on high-stakes tests like the APs, PBL students perform as well as traditionally taught students—or better.[3] Research also shows PBL students are stronger problem-solvers, and better able to apply their learning to real-life situations.[4] They score higher on skills related to critical thinking, and—this might be the most compelling of all—they *care* more.[5] For any parent or teacher who has struggled to motivate a teenager to do their work, what projects can do to inspire them is huge. PBL classrooms have better attendance, and students who are more engaged. Students who are struggling are also more engaged by project-based learning, making it a promising strategy for *all* students, not just those who are already thriving.[6] Teachers, too, are more motivated by PBL, describing themselves as more satisfied with their jobs.[7] It does not require a study to show that having happier teachers is a good thing for kids.

Preparing our kids to be adults means preparing them to make good decisions when they're out in the world, which research shows is PBL's strength. A group of researchers out of the University of Chicago conducted a study of fifth graders where some were taught the material by direct instruction (with their teacher orchestrating a class activity, plus independent work at their seat), and some worked on a project using the exact same course materials. When the unit was finished, the students were given a completely unrelated, complex problem about whether to tell the teacher about another student's dishonesty. They were asked to write an essay about what they would do and why. The researchers were looking for the following in the essays: 1) Did the students weigh multiple sides of the dilemma?; 2) How many types of reasons and moral principles did they consider?; and 3) How explicitly did they weigh different options?—all indicators of strong decision-making. PBL students performed far better, as they "considered more than one side of a dilemma, used more comprehensive reasoning, and more frequently evaluated the importance of the assumptions underlying their decision making."[8]

FLASHY, NOT DEEP

As a high school teacher, I taught a few interdisciplinary projects to my students, and I'd seen firsthand how students
benefited. One project asked each student to select a historical figure, do in-depth research on the person, and then construct the contents and narrative around the "trunk" that
person would have carried when they came to America.
When I designed the project, I assumed some students might
feel inspired and create some sketches of what was in the
trunk, but I was mostly focused on the research and writing.
As it happened, the students became deeply interested in
their historical figures. Their research unearthed facts and
stories I hadn't imagined (*Do you know the type of medical and
mental health tests immigrants on Ellis Island were subjected to?*).
Discussions were engaging and lively and kids seemed to be
making connections between the novels we were reading,
history, and their own lives. Kids called their grandparents to
find out more about the stories they'd heard, but hadn't paid
attention to, and others questioned the accuracy of the history portrayed in a popular movie of the time.

Kasey's project was particularly compelling. I don't remember the character, but I remember her presentation. She
brought in an actual trunk filled with artifacts her historical
person would have had. She dressed like her historical figure
and gave an impassioned and compelling narrative from the
figure's point of view. When we debriefed afterward, she admitted she had never liked history. She didn't understand the
relevance of it. It always seemed stale, and felt like just a se-

ries of facts. However, when we combined history with literature and looked at it through the lens of the American Dream, it gave her a way to make sense of it. She was deeply impacted by the stories of people, and the opportunity to approach history that way had made her curious. She dug in to learn more, which helped her connect everything back to why any of it mattered. She was particularly compelled by our tracing of the American Dream. She was a beautiful, popular girl who lived in a nice home in suburban America in the late 1990s. She began to wonder, what's next? Is this it? Am I supposed to try to have the same life my parents have? What about all of these other people who don't have this?

I loved this project and the spark I saw it ignite in my students. At the same time, I knew I was missing the mark, something I see with much more clarity now. What specific skills was I helping students develop with this project? What was I assessing? Did this project prepare them to do college-level analysis? The truth is, I didn't really have a handle on it. My trunk project had all of the flashy bells and whistles, but lacked enough substance. I hadn't been building skills over the years through project after project. It was a one-off. It was dessert. The fact is, as an individual teacher, I had neither the time nor the support to build out a meaningful project. I could see the potential in project-based learning, but couldn't bring it fully to life by myself.

OBSTACLES: TEXTBOOKS, ACCOUNTABILITY, AND NOSTALGIA

One of the opportunities we had at Summit was to work as a team to build a curriculum that was project-based. I was committed, as was every teacher we hired. We quickly realized one of the reasons schools everywhere haven't adopted PBL—it was incredibly hard and complex to do. It's not easy to design a project that cuts across subject areas, is academically rigorous, engaging, and speaks to what students need to learn to satisfy state standards. We searched for ready-made, proven projects we could adopt, and the few we found were extremely expensive. Two organizations offered a PBL curriculum, but to use them you had to pay thousands of dollars a year to be part of their networks. One company would design them for us, but they cost about $10,000 per project and we wouldn't even own them or be able to share them. For the most part, we ended up developing our own, and we engaged our teachers directly in this challenging work. Our teachers' work ultimately extended into a few summers, so we could expand, evolve, and continually improve our project-based curriculum. Working in teams, they pulled from the strongest projects in their own personal collections and created new projects aligned to the important skills and habits we needed to develop in our kids. It was the collective brainpower I'd been missing when I was a teacher. The process was time intensive, and it made sense to me why these outside companies charged so much.

The lack of availability of quality projects is a clear obstacle to widespread adoption of PBL. In the place of projects, we have textbooks, which, it will come as no surprise, are not project-based. We are a culture steeped in standards and accountability. Textbook companies need to get their books purchased, but to do so, they have to show how every single grade-level standard and test item is covered in their books and materials. If I'm a textbook publisher, I'm incentivized to make that as clear and easy as possible. Need to learn about how a bill becomes a law? See pages 40–42, and be sure to memorize the diagram, as you are likely to be tested on it. This is much more straightforward than creating a Congressional Simulation project—as we ultimately did at Summit— that asks each student to assume the persona of a real lawmaker who selects an issue, researches it, and proposes a bill, all the while considering what it means to be an effective and ethical legislator. The textbook approach may be more standardized and straightforward, but it doesn't ask kids to think deeply, make connections, or solve problems. "How a bill becomes a law" becomes an individual, disconnected piece of information, something a student will likely forget once the test is over.

The standardized test is another clear obstacle to PBL. Trying something different brings uncertainty. Test scores drive school rankings and, ultimately, property values. Parents work hard—often financially stretching themselves—to buy houses and live in top-performing school districts and, once there, fight hard to keep up their school's reputation. And PBL feels to many—teachers, principals, and parents— like a risk. So they teach the familiar way, the way they've always taught. I find it ironic, because the purpose of standardized tests is to show how students perform and how prepared they are, and yet these tests get in the way of the best way *to* prepare them. Even more ironic is the fact that PBL kids do well on standardized tests.

A teacher or principal might love the idea of PBL, or might have had an experience like my trunk project where they saw how their students benefited. It's one thing to love it, and another to be willing to fight for it. At the end of the day, they're accountable for their school rankings. If they use the textbooks, materials, and tests supplied to them and yet don't meet their targeted scores, they can reasonably say, "Hey, I did my best with what you gave me." But if they go out on a limb, if they choose a different approach, the finger points just to them. (Yes, it's hard to be a teacher.) This is why we so often get the dessert version of PBL. Teachers try desperately to do what they are supposed to do and, at the same time, what they believe is best for their students.

There aren't a lot of parents out rallying for PBL, either. After all, most of us learned in the traditional way, and we turned out fine. Yes, school can be hard and boring, we reason, but part of life is learning how to do hard and boring things sometimes. So, like the teachers and principals, we focus on making sure our kids get the right grades because that's what matters for the next step: getting into college. There's a tricky psychology at play when it comes to school. Everyone who went through school (which is most people) has a bias and perspective about what it should be. We can't help it. We're human and we generalize our schooling and experience. Educators certainly do it. Most did well in school, or at least felt comfortable there.

Parents ground themselves in what is familiar, their own experience, and can often be heard saying, "I turned out fine, so it must be okay for my child." Even if they acknowledge their school experience was substandard in some way, they believe "it built character." That may be true. But if we can piece apart the nostalgia around football games and the bonding experience of commiserating with classmates about boredom in math class, what is there? It's difficult, if you're generally happy with your life, to think, "What if my education had been better?" Would that have been a bad thing? If you got to where you are now faster, or with less boredom and busywork and more time for exploration, interests, and relationships, what else might you have been able to accomplish? Knowingly or not, it is our unwillingness to honestly engage with these questions that often blocks change.

Further, what parents are most interested in, understandably, is getting their own child through the system. School might not be perfect, but at least they know how to navigate it, and with everything else they have going on, figuring out an entirely new way to "do school" is far from ideal. So we say, "Buckle down. Do your homework, memorize how a bill becomes a law so you can do well on the test." We might shrug in agreement when our kid tells us it's boring, reminding them, "You've got to play the game sometimes." In the back of our mind, though, is fear, the idea that, at the end of the day, they've only got one shot.

REAL-WORLD LEARNING IN REAL LIFE

An instructor gave my son, Rett, a little white uniform during his one-on-one orientation. The brief introduction was all he knew about Tae Kwon Do when he joined his first class. I took a seat in the back with the other parents and looked on as the the class started stretching. Legs apart, bend over and touch the floor. This quickly shifted to sliding your feet out. Lots of the kids did the splits. Rett couldn't even touch his fingers to the ground when he bent over. I sat in the back, wringing my hands and wondering if I'd made the right choice. How in the world would he ever be able to do what these other kids were doing? Next they started practicing basic punches and kicks. The instructor demonstrated and then began calling out instruction. Many kids followed with ease. Others got some, but not all, and Rett just stood and watched for a moment. Soon, a TA stood beside him, showing him step-by-step what to do and then asking him to try. Every time he messed up or got stuck he paused and watched the others until he could rejoin. I watched as other students and the instructor helped him throughout the class. At the end, he got his first belt . . . the white "novice" belt. Even the tying of the belt seemed difficult to me. It went so fast— how did they do that? But the expectation was simple: come back, wear your uniform, bring your belt, we'll help you tie it, just try again.

Outside of school, activities like this one offer incredible opportunity for real-world-style learning. But not all after-school activities are created equal. When I started looking for a martial arts program, I noticed that most took more of the traditional schooling approach, where the focus was on kids advancing and competing. In class, they would learn discrete skills that, once demonstrated, equaled advancement to the next belt, with an ultimate goal of earning a black belt. Classes also focused on preparing kids for competitions, which are a lot like standardized tests. The competitions have winners and losers, and there are specific ways to score points and then win. But the way you score a point has almost nothing in common with how you would act in a real-life situation if you were trying to escape a fight or defend yourself. In other words, they're not very real-world. How often are you going to be on a mat, sized to a competitor who is your same skill and age? Who is going to attack you no matter what you do or say, but can only hit you in a few discrete parts of your body?

We chose a dojo for Rett that's all about real-world application of Tae Kwon Do. To be clear, there are colored belts and lots of kicking and punching, but there are many differences. The classes are mixed age, mixed skill, and mixed gender, so the students are constantly exposed to people who are more experienced, and others who are less experienced . . . like real life. If a student decides to compete, it's his choice and he takes on additional work to specially prepare, but that's not the focus of the class. Instead, class is geared toward understanding Tae Kwon Do in our everyday life, learning things like de-escalation, understanding one's individual skills and strengths, working as a group to achieve a goal, learning to breathe, requesting feedback, and contributing to the community. Earning a black belt is the beginning and not the end, and students are expected to teach others during their black belt "questing year" and beyond. Today Rett is a black belt and is teaching classes for kids who started exactly where he did.

The parallels to our students' performance on the Sim City project are undeniable. The underlying goal of projects is to help kids be better prepared for the world. Unlike a standardized test or Tae Kwon Do competition, life today has fewer and fewer clearly defined, straightforward tasks a person completes to win or advance. Rather, life is messy and complicated, and you have to figure out what's needed at any given time, and what you can bring—then do *that*. Employers are looking for kids who grow up to be adults who, when starting a job, have the problem-solving skills and confidence to get their feet under them. Parents want children who, when they lose a job unexpectedly, can assess what steps they need to take next. Everyone wins when kids become adults who, when they are embarking on things like a major move, or welcoming twin babies, know how to work with their partner to share responsibilities and get it all done. Our communities need adults who, when they encounter a complex moral issue, have the decision-making skills to contemplate both sides, apply different types of reasoning, and question assumptions. Kids don't want to just recite how a bill becomes a law (if they happen to remember it), they want to know what it feels like and takes to push an issue through that is important to them. They want to be prepared for life as much as we want them to be.

Chapter Five

Self-Direction:
The Fallacy of Sink or Swim

Maybe it was the hype, but what was supposed to be the best lab in chemistry—actually the *only* fun lab of the year—was a total bust. When I was a student we all liked Mr. Mathews, but none of us liked chemistry. With his wild Albert Einstein hair and thick glasses, he looked the part of the mad scientist chemistry teacher, but in reality there wasn't much mad science going on. We spent most of our time listening to lectures, taking notes, memorizing the periodic table, and solving equations. From time to time we shifted from the desks in the center of the room to the lab tables on the sides and worked our way through intricate directions to complete lab experiments.

On this last day of school in December, ready for vacation and high on sugar, my lab-mates and I flipped to page 3 of the step-by-step direction sheet for the experiment that was supposed to provide us with a holiday surprise. There wasn't much that was experimental. As with all of our labs, Mr. Mathews had spent countless hours measuring and labeling every ingredient we needed and carefully laying out the instruments to be used. Our job was simply to follow the instructions like they were a recipe from a beginner's cookbook.

Maybe if we had known the purpose of the lab, or what we were trying to accomplish, we could have recognized things weren't coming together as they should. Perhaps we could have problem-solved or even asked for help at the right moment. But we didn't know where we were headed or why, and so we just kept going until we reached the final step. One of my partners said, "Check the back. There's got to be more." Another wondered if this was the April Fools' Day lab, not the Christmas lab. We looked around at the other tables to see if anyone had something different, but table after table was filled with confused high school sophomores staring at a runny, sugary mess with a few peanuts floating around in it.

Mr. Mathews scampered from one lab table to another, muttering to himself, checking the lab sheet and the chemicals and then the lab sheet again. The bell rang and we all sort of stared at him, unsure of what to do or what he expected. Finally, a student asked, "Mr. Mathews, what was it supposed to be?" His shoulders visibly slumped. His face crestfallen, he answered, "Peanut brittle. A holiday treat."

It was a teaching gimmick. It backfired, but I sometimes wonder what it would have accomplished even if we had succeeded in making perfect peanut brittle from Mr. Mathews's instructions. Would it have inspired any of us to be chemists (none of us went that route) or chemistry majors (none of us were)? Would it have motivated us to study harder or to get better grades? Or, for some, to show up on time to the 8 a.m. class? We'll never know those answers for sure, but we can reasonably presume it wouldn't have changed much at all.

Nearly thirty years later, I thought of Mr. Mathews as I talked with a group of Summit high school students. Our conversation had covered all sorts of ground as I checked in with them about their experience, what was working well, what could be improved, and what ideas they had to make things better. It was a passing comment from one student, Ethan—"I'm taking the AP Chemistry exam"—that caught my attention.

"Wait, what did you say?" I asked, confused and curious.

"I'm taking the AP Chemistry exam in a few weeks."

"But we don't offer AP Chem," I protested.

"Oh, I know," he said, seeing the source of my confusion. "A group of us really like chemistry and we wanted to learn more about it, so we decided to create our own AP Chemistry study group and teach it to ourselves." He looked as if that explanation should do the trick and got ready to move back to our previous conversation.

I kept my voice low and casual, knowing I would get more if I didn't get too excited or surprised. "That sounds interesting. Can you tell me how you went about that?"

"Sure," he said with a shrug. "Well, like I said, there's a group of us who just really like chemistry. The projects are really cool and interesting and so we wanted to learn more about it. So a few of us set that as one of our annual goals. I mean, we wanted to explore if this is something we want to keep going with. We figured the best way for us to show what we learned, since there isn't a class with a grade, was to take the AP exam. So we made a plan to start a study group. We got an AP Chem book, and Khan Academy, and a bunch of other resources, and then, you know, we just organized our learning into projects and playlists. We already know how to learn, so we just followed the same approach we have in our other classes and created a plan. We applied to do an independent study and it was approved, so we're working through our plan, learning and preparing for the test. Ms. Compton, our chemistry teacher, has been our mentor and helped us set our goals and develop our plans. We check in with her and she gives us feedback. She even introduced us to some people who are chemists so we can understand how they use what we're learning in their real jobs."

"And so what's your reflection on the experience?" I asked.

"Well," he said, "I learned a lot about what I like and some things I don't like. For example, I like hypothesizing and experimenting. I really like it when science is used to solve real problems. I'm less interested in spending years and years working in a lab on one idea or theory. And we'll see how I do on the AP exam. I know from the feedback and all of the diagnostics I've taken that I've learned a ton, we'll just see how that translates on a bubble exam, but I feel good about it no matter what."

When I told that story at a barbecue a few days later, a mother immediately responded, "Oh, that level of independence would *never* work for my son. He needs far more structure. He would never be able to do something like that on his own." It's a comment I hear often—all the time, in fact—when I'm talking with parents about the self-direction we teach, and expect, at Summit. Whenever I hear this comment, I wonder, when *do* we give kids independence? And how do they learn what to do with it?

TEACHING VERSUS LEARNING

For well over a hundred years, American schools have had this basic premise: kids need to know certain information before they become adults. The job of the school is to teach it and the job of the student is to learn it. The other job of the school is to show the world the student learned it. The approach is pretty simple. Basically a teacher presents the information to a group of students using a lecture, text, film, or any other methods they see fit. The student internalizes, studies, and practices the knowledge, then shows they know it on an exam. The exam is scored, the student is ranked via a grade, and the class moves on.

If only it were that simple. For the vast majority of students, learning from lectures and textbooks is not only boring, but ineffective. It probably always was, but today when you can watch a YouTube video on how to do anything and Google everything, students are particularly unmotivated to sit through static lectures, take notes, and make flash cards. The science of learning is pretty clear that almost any student can master similar levels of material, but they do so at different paces and using different processes. We also know that what they learn will stay with them longer if it is presented in a familiar framework and applied to a real-life context. They aren't wrong to dislike the approach to learning they find in most of their classes. The evidence is clear it doesn't work for most people.

Teachers, then, have two jobs that are in opposition to each other. On the one hand, they are responsible for students' learning. This is obvious, I know. It's also what motivated most teachers to enter the profession in the first place, and one of the things they love about their job. Their second responsibility is ensuring students' grades show what the student has done, and that they grade their students in a fair and ethical way. Many would say, "Aren't those connected, though? Teachers help students learn, then students get good grades." But this is a false correlation because the system of evaluation is so deeply flawed. Grades offer little in the way of objectivity, as two-thirds of teachers acknowledge their grading reflects progress, effort, and participation in class. Grades offer little consistency, as grading rigor varies from teacher to teacher and from school to school. And grades offer little in the way of specificity; most parents and some students don't know the reasoning behind a letter grade.

Teachers are also really constrained in how they do their work, by the number of students they have, the amount of time they see them, the materials they have access to, and what they are expected to teach. When you put all of this together, what you end up with is a daily struggle for the teacher to get enough students to show up, be on time, pay attention, and learn enough, long enough, to get a passing grade and do well enough on the exam. The student struggle is to hold on to a longer-term objective, be it graduation from high school or acceptance to college, to stay motivated through the daily grind.

Everyone's acting rationally, and yet none of it actually makes sense. We end up with a majority of kids who have only learned parts of the information we tried to teach them. Along the way they've become disengaged, unmotivated, and burned out, even if they do get the score or the grade. We end up with teachers who have become disillusioned and frustrated when they are unable to do what they entered the profession to do. They either leave teaching, or look for small wins in the form of individual students who succeed.

What we don't end up with is an entire class of students leaving high school with the knowledge they need to move into adulthood but, more important, with the ability to be learners for the rest of their lives. In our rapidly changing world, there is no possible way for a human to know all they need to know for next year, let alone for a lifetime, by the time they turn eighteen. But few schools teach to this reality. That's what we had to change when we created Summit.

BUILDING ON THE WORK OF OTHERS

I'm a research junkie, as are most of my colleagues. Reading the work of Daniel Pink, Angela Duckworth, and Linda Darling-Hammond informed how we thought about learning, and how we did our jobs. At Summit we had a "leadership bookshelf," a set of books we all read, discussed, learned from, and then sought to incorporate.

Daniel Pink's bestselling *Drive* was one of the books on our bookshelf, as it shared research pointing to mastery, autonomy, and purpose as the underpinnings of motivation. Simply put, mastery is when you become good at something, autonomy is when you have some measure of control, and purpose is when you're doing something for a reason that is authentic to you. We read Pink's work, and thought, what if we designed learning with mastery, autonomy, and purpose at the center? Today, we call it self-directed learning. What it means is students become the leaders of their own learning. What it takes is years of deliberate practice and feedback, intentionally building the skills to do so.

I befriended David Yeager, a protégé of the great psychologist Carol Dweck (whose research helped the world understand the importance of the growth—versus fixed—mindset). David came to visit one of our schools, and after looking around for a few hours, he sat down with us to talk. We explained how we wanted our students to commit to a plan, and to set goals for themselves in a meaningful way and with meaningful guideposts. We wanted them to learn how to be self-directed when we weren't there to guide them. He started talking and narrated what became our *self-directed learning cycle*.

Dweck has shown that deliberate practice in the art of short-, medium-, and long-term goal-setting supports students' development and attainment of a sense of purpose.[1] So as a first step, Summit students set a goal that's rooted in a sense of purpose. It might be something like using evidence to support an argumentative claim, or managing their time so they won't cram to complete a three-week project the night before it's due. Then they make a plan for how they're going to reach that goal. Next is the implementation of that plan—this is the part where they learn/*do*. As they work, they check in with themselves and their mentor, making sure they're on track and employing self-directed behaviors as needed. They may need to shift their strategy, find appropriate help, or seek more challenge. Then, when they're finished, they must show what they know. This might look like a performance, or a completed product. The next step is to reflect on what went well and why, and what was hard, and why. Finally, they rinse and repeat. They go through the same cycle again in the next class, and the class after that. The role of the adults in the room is to answer questions and help guide, but without taking control.

We drafted this cycle in that room with David in an hour, sketching it on a whiteboard. That afternoon helped us recognize that it wasn't enough to just read these great thinkers' papers and books. Researchers and practitioners needed to come together and hear one another. So we didn't stop with David. We started cold-calling researchers, including many of the authors of the books on our leadership bookshelf, and introducing ourselves. Though it may seem brazen, we said, "Here's our design. Can you help? What are we missing? What are we getting wrong? Where are we on the mark?" And incredibly, they responded, helping us course-correct our self-directed learning cycle to become what it is today.

The good news is that self-direction can be learned. The mom at the barbecue was probably right that her son didn't have the skills to be self-directed, but her answer to that was to keep him in environments that imposed more and more structure, so he would never have to use self-directed skills. In actuality, what he probably needs *most* is intensive development of those skills. After all, if he doesn't learn them now, while he has the support of a family and school, when will he learn them? College? His first job? When he lives on his own?

It had taken years of practice for our student Ethan to apply the cycle to creating an entire chemistry learning experience for himself and others. But he didn't start that way. He started by learning the cycle in the context of a single hour. And then doing it again the next hour. And the next.

SETTING GOALS

"What is your goal for this period? You have two minutes. Go!" The whiteboard wall projected a timer counting down to zero, next to a "SMART goal" framework. SMART goals, developed by George Doran, Arthur Miller, and James Cunningham, are Specific, Measurable, Actionable, Realistic, and Timebound. "Make it SMART," reminded Ms. Jones. It was *self-directed learning time,* a dedicated hour each day of school for students to work independently, with peers, or with their teacher, on anything from French Revolution causes to complex numbers and rational exponents, based on their personal goals and what they needed to accomplish that day or week. While it sounds a bit like study hall, self-directed learning time is fundamentally different. What the student is working on is driven by the overall learning objectives from the projects, but the day-to-day learning is driven by goals set by the student in consultation with his or her mentor. So perhaps a student's goal by the end of the week is to master a particular math concept. The self-directed learning time teacher knows that, the mentor knows that, the math teacher knows that, the student knows that—because all of this information is available in a snapshot through the platform we created. The student can choose to use their time to work toward that goal or another goal.

Ms. Jones circulated the room asking specific questions as each student worked on his or her laptop.

"Is that realistic for sixty minutes or do you need to adjust?"

"Where is the time in your goal? When will you complete the goal?"

"When I read that and don't know what's in your head, it doesn't tell me what you're going to specifically do."

"When you have a draft," she called to the room as the timer ticked down, "share it with a partner and get some feedback. Make adjustments."

When the two minutes were up, Ms. Jones said, "Okay, let's share them, so we can make informed plans and hold each other accountable." She projected a shared document the kids had all added their goals to, so everyone could see everyone else's. "Take a look at these goals, and as you think about your own goal and plan to achieve it, are there any resources in your class you can access? Is anyone working on a similar goal?"

She paused a moment, then said, "We'll take two minutes to make our plans. What are you trying to achieve? What resources do you have? What do you know about yourself and how you work best? Detail it out. Step-by-step. Go." Within the two minutes, plans took shape for every student, each customized, but with common features. Many wanted to master what we call a "focus area," but they ranged in subjects. Their plans included things like taking a diagnostic assessment to understand what they already knew about the subject, reviewing all of the objectives and vocabulary they were expected to know, or watching a crash course video on the topic. Some students' plans included studying with a partner who was working on the same goal, explaining it to each other, doing some practice problems, and checking each other's work.

Less than eight minutes into the hour, every student was off to enact their plan for the hour. Some worked independently, others in small groups, and a few in pairs. Some had earphones on and hoods up. Some sat in chairs, others on the floor, and a few even found space under a table. Every ten minutes a volunteer timekeeper for the day announced the time remaining. As the time wound down, students began to accomplish their goals, which were still projected on the whiteboard screen. As they clicked "done," the goal turned green and classmates said, "Congratulations! Nice work," or applauded before returning to their work. One student who had been trying to master a science concept for some time received several high fives and a shoulder bump hug when he achieved his goal. The other kids knew he'd been working on it for a while and so really understood the power of this achievement.

With seven minutes left in the period Ms. Jones brought the class back together. "Let's reflect on this last hour and our goal cycle. What went well and why?"

"I finished my goal just in time," said David with a big grin as he scanned his classmates for affirmation.

"So I understand that finishing your goal is positive. Why is doing it just in time good?"

A bit more seriously, he said, "Well, I worked the entire time and so I think it means I set a goal that was right for me. I'm starting to get to know how long it takes me to do stuff, so I can plan my time better."

"Powerful knowledge to have about yourself. Thanks for sharing. Who else set a goal that was the right size for them?" Several hands shot up.

"What else went well?"

"I've been struggling with linear equations and inequalities," said Sasha. "I've missed my goals on it a few times. The stuff I normally do hasn't been working, so today I saw that Ingrid and Raj had it as their goal and so we formed a study group. That really helped me, working with them. I figured out what I didn't understand and I hit my goal today, finally."

"Sounds like you exhibited one of the five power behaviors of a self-directed learner, strategy-shifting. You recognized that what you normally do wasn't getting you to your goal and so you rethought your plan and shifted strategies. Nice."

Ms. Jones—like all Summit teachers—reinforces the *five power behaviors* often throughout the day. Those five behaviors are strategy-shifting, challenge-seeking, persistence, responding to setbacks, and appropriate help-seeking. Ms.

Jones addressed the class again. "What didn't work well and why?"

"I didn't make my goal," said Kyle, his shoulders a bit slumped.

"While that doesn't feel great, what did you learn from it?"

His expression shifted from gloomy to curious. "Um, I made my goal mastering cells, but I hadn't looked at it at all, so I didn't realize it's pretty complicated. I've been doing really well on my other bio content, so I guess I got overconfident. When I took the diagnostic, I realized I didn't know anything. So I kinda got frustrated. I knew I wasn't going to make it this period, so I didn't really work as hard as I normally do."

"Thanks for being honest. What's your takeaway from the last sixty minutes? What can you take into your next hour to improve?"

"I think I wasted some time," Kyle said, "because I knew I wasn't going to make my goal. Maybe I should have changed my goal when I figured out I wasn't going to make it this period. Maybe that would have motivated me more."

"That is definitely a strategy you could have employed. It sounds like realizing you weren't going to make your goal this period was a mental setback for you. I hear in your reflection a realization that your response to that setback could have been more productive. Rather than accepting you weren't going to meet your goal and not using your time as well as you could have, your response to the setback could have been to redefine your goal in light of the new information and then go after that goal with all you have.

"You all have identified two of the five power behaviors of a self-directed learner," Ms. Jones continued, "strategy-shifting and responding to setbacks. Did anyone display any of the other three in this last hour?"

"Gabe did," said Anna. "He asked me a really specific question about the industrial revolution. He understood most of it, but was confused about one part. I think that was appropriate help-seeking because he'd done the work to know what he didn't know and he wasn't asking me to do it for him."

"I think most of us showed persistence today," said Todd. "I mean, we were working hard for the entire period, and look how many people achieved their goals. And those aren't easy goals."

"I agree," said Ms. Jones. "What about challenge-seekers? Anyone show the challenge-seeking behavior today?"

"I did," said Cooper. "I hate math. I'm terrible at it. But the project we're working on is pretty interesting and I need to know some stuff for it, so today I decided to start with math. So I made it my first goal."

CLASSROOM BUFFET

Summit students often aren't all sitting at desks facing the teacher, but rather scattered about doing work they have planned and are controlling. Parents raise their eyebrows at this. Often implied, but rarely stated, is a belief that this doesn't sound like kids are doing the hard work of learning. It's as if I've opened up a free-for-all, all-you-can-eat classroom buffet. They imagine kids gorging themselves on carbs and desserts, or Instagram and video games. They have a hard time imagining kids would make good, healthy choices on their own.

I think of it more like the buffet they offer at Google. At the Google buffet, all of the foods on offer are marked with clear red, yellow, and green signs. If something is green, it's healthy and should be eaten every day of the week. (Think salads, fruits, healthy grains, lean proteins.) If it's yellow, it's good to eat a couple of times a week, but you don't want to go completely nuts, either. (Cheese-heavy things might fall into this category, types of meat, and pasta.) And if it's red, the message is "Be careful with this." (Doughnuts!) The portions are thoughtful, though you can certainly get more than one portion. The plates are small to discourage taking more than you need. Cooks walk around talking to diners about the food, answering their questions, and just generally offering information.

This is the buffet we offer kids at Summit. We help curate their experience and give them strong guidance and informed suggestions. They don't scroll through YouTube and say, "Hmm, what do I want to learn today?" Rather, they set goals with their mentor and choose from a range of ways to get there that we have culled for them and are directly in service to the projects they are working on. Teachers spend their time on high-value pursuits, answering questions, giving feedback, and engaging in conversations that are meaningful to the development of students. We offer a four-star buffet experience, not an all-night, all-you-can-eat extravaganza, and not a no-substitutions, no-replacements pre-plated meal the kid has no say in. That doesn't mean it always looks like Ms. Jones's self-directed learning hour. Sometimes it looks really messy.

PRODUCTIVE FAILURE

Skill development is lumpy and it takes time and practice for kids to set a SMART goal and make a viable plan. During rough spots, and with technology readily available, kids get distracted. They watch a video, play a game, text a friend, or otherwise waste time they should spend learning.

Will was an extreme example of a kid who made bad choices. During his first three weeks at Summit, he didn't do anything during self-directed learning time. Literally, nothing. He wasn't disruptive. He sat quietly, computer open, a learning tab open. When anyone walked by he pretended to read, or would bring his hands to the keyboard as if he was typing. In meetings with his mentor he set goals, but with a lot of help, then did nothing to move toward meeting even one of his goals. Will's teachers knew this, his mentor knew this, and I knew this. We talked often about what was going on with him and what we should do. We knew from his records that he had been passed from grade to grade by scraping by, and often only after attending summer school. He wasn't a disruptive presence, but rather had seemed to figure out—at least at his previous schools—how to do the minimum, at the very last moment, and still get swept up with the rest of the class to the next grade level.

I was curious about Will, and started watching him and

sitting in on his classes. During one self-directed hour, he called me over. Apparently, I wasn't a good spy. He was wondering about something. He knew I was "in charge" and he thought I might be able to help him. Unlike in all of his previous school experiences, he wasn't moving forward. There wasn't a teacher who was telling him to move on to the next thing, he said, so nothing *moved*. What did that mean? he wondered.

It was such a profound moment for me, to watch this kid stumble his way through what really was an epiphany. What Will had realized was that he had to engage, that he had to do something or he wasn't going to learn anything. Previously he had mistaken the movement of the class for his own movement. As we talked it became clear to me he had no idea what it meant to actually learn something and the role he had to play in order to learn. School had never been about learning to him. It was just about getting through. This wasn't a magic wand moment, where all of a sudden he began to apply himself and within months became a stellar student. Rather, the next few years involved tons of work from all of us. But it had been a crucial breakthrough and made the work possible.

The more profound breakthrough for me, though, was when I talked about this kid with educators from outside Summit. Rather than seeing the story as I did, as a huge leap forward in his learning, they were appalled. "How could you have let this kid sit there for three weeks and accomplish nothing?" Many accused me of the equivalent of malpractice.

At first I thought I hadn't told the story correctly. He had been accomplishing nothing for his entire education—he'd turned avoidance into an art. The fact that it took him three weeks to have an epiphany about the role of autonomy in his education was well worth it. Now we had a chance of doing something different for most of high school, before he left and floundered in the "real world." It hadn't been wasted time at all—he'd spent a lifetime being swept up in the momentum of the system. It was going to take a minute for him to recognize that. But adults so often feel if a kid is struggling, we have to pick them up immediately, and so many debates about our approach with Will ended in a stalemate.

Ultimately, the experience with Will helped me understand people have a complicated relationship with failure. Most of us fear it for ourselves, and for our kids. But we also know kids are supposed to learn from failure. So how do we find the sweet spot?

SINK OR SWIM

When I was about four years old, my family went on our first vacation. We piled into our station wagon and drove south to Los Angeles, where both of my parents had family. The drive was hot and dusty. There was no air-conditioning and so by the time we reached the Motel 6 where we were staying, the simple concrete pool looked like an oasis. I remember being excited by the novelty of sleeping somewhere other than home and the prospect of the cool water. I didn't know how to swim. My only exposure to water had been a lake with a shallow shore that allowed for active play without needing to swim. The Motel 6 pool didn't have a shallow end, so my mother wouldn't allow me to go in without an adult, but she was busy watching my sister. My dad didn't want to go in, and his solution was "You have to learn sometime." As I sat on the edge dangling my feet in, I remember him saying, "She'll either sink or swim," as he scooped me up from under my arms and dropped me in the deep end before I realized what was happening. I still remember how loud it sounded, as if I was crashing into something, as my head broke through the water. It was unlikely I would have learned to swim in that moment; after all, I didn't have any skills or training and, at age four, any instincts I had to float were likely overridden by panic and fear. I remember the terrifying feeling of breathing in water and the wavy view of the bottom, as I helplessly thrashed and kicked while sinking. There was another splash and a violent jerk on the back of my suit as my mother jumped in and saved me. Though I eventually learned to swim, the process was harder than it should have been. The pool incident had left me petrified of the water and convinced I was a terrible swimmer, two scars I contend with to this day.

While the basic idea of learning from failure is supported by evidence, the sink-or-swim method doesn't really work. Failing is only productive when two things are true: first, the person who fails actually learns something from it and is thus motivated to try again; and second, the failure doesn't permanently close future doors.

When it comes to our children, we tend to wonder which is better—let them fail, or not?—when there's an obvious challenge ahead, like a test. The problem is, while failing a test or a course won't result in death like drowning will, it nevertheless feels terrifying for kids and parents. Real conse-

quences loom: graduation, college acceptance, and even getting reasonable car insurance (which, at least in California, is
cheaper for students with a B average or higher). These con-
sequences are daunting enough that many parents intervene
to prevent failure. But it doesn't stop there. We want to avoid
nearing the crisis point to begin with because it is so stressful, and so we naturally start putting structures in place to
prevent our kids from even coming close to a failure. And
before we know it, we have elaborate systems and structures
for checking homework, monitoring grades and assignments,
contacting teachers, even checking up on class participation.

Teachers don't want kids to fail, either, and so they offer
extra credit for meaningless work to allow for passing grades.
They also credit "effort" in their grades, problematic because
it keeps the student moving along when really they might be
falling further and further behind. Schools offer summer
school courses that are more about attendance than learning.
The intentions are right. No one wants our kids to fail out of
school. But nor do we want kids who are dependent upon
others to structure everything for them.

Ironically, video games, one of the things parents often
fight against in their quest to prevent failure, offer some real
insight into a third way. When Rett was ten, he would do
anything to get his hands on my phone to play Cut the Rope.
An app that was getting rave reviews, Cut the Rope was
based on the science and math principles of angles and veloc-
ity, so I downloaded it and shared it with Rett as a treat. In
the game, an adorable little monster named Om Nom loves
candy. In order for him to get it, the player has to cut the rope

that the candy dangles from in exactly the right place so that it falls into Om Nom's mouth. Sounds easy, but it gets pretty hard, pretty quickly, with all sorts of imaginative contraptions that must be figured out to deliver the candy. The second I handed the phone to Rett he was off, going so fast I couldn't even follow his moves.

"Slow down!" I protested. "I can't even see what you're doing!"

"What, Mom? I'm just playing it the way you're supposed to."

What I quickly realized is that he was cutting the rope in the wrong place, a lot. Om Nom was sad every time, but Rett didn't waste time worrying about it. As I sat back and watched, it became clear Rett wasn't fazed by the failure. He had realized it didn't matter, and so he tested and retested, figuring out as he did where to cut next. His approach was methodical and strategic, and really fast. Unencumbered by the fear of failure, he could progress through the game rapidly, getting better with each attempt, incorporating as much learning from the misses as the successes.

ONE MEAL A WEEK

When Rett started at Summit a couple of years later, he got similar small opportunities to fail every time he went through the self-directed cycle in class. He would set his goal, make his plan, do the work, and sometimes he would meet the goal, sometimes not. I wanted to emulate the cycle at home, too, so Scott and I tested it around cooking dinner. My family—including Rett—is passionate about food. We're a little obsessed, actually. We love eating, we love talking about food, we love cooking it. When Rett turned thirteen, I thought, *Hmm, he's old enough to learn how to prepare dinner. There's no reason he can't do that.* After we made a compelling argument that included our purposely exaggerated skepticism about whether he would get any dinner on Wednesdays if he didn't make it himself, he agreed he wanted to learn how to cook. We reasoned that even if he just learned to make ten things by the time he was eighteen, he'd leave our house knowing how to make ten meals for himself, and he could definitely survive like that. He liked the idea of having a meal a week that he had total control of.

I didn't set him loose and say, "Okay, great, call me when dinner's ready!" We are both pretty sure he would have failed. Instead, I went through a bunch of recipes and pulled out the ones I thought would be good for him to start on, the ones without a ton of ingredients or really complicated steps and techniques. (The Google buffet!) From that curated pile, he chose what he wanted to make that week, and we all shopped for ingredients for the week together.

I made a few mistakes at first. I got distracted and disappeared while Rett was cooking—he needed guidance, and without it, burned something. I got too involved. He didn't know proper knife techniques so when he almost cut his finger I rushed in and before we knew it, I was cooking and he was watching. There was some foundational knowledge he was missing, like why the order of adding ingredients matters. But I also couldn't go in and do it for him. This was really tempting, because on the nights he cooked, dinner took a long time. The kitchen became messier than I'd like, and quite frankly the food was not as good. I hadn't realized that twenty years of practice translated to vegetables that were crisp, not mushy, and nicely browned meats. And as an experienced cook things take a lot less time for me to do than Rett, who is a beginner. But I noticed that if Rett asked me a question and my answer turned into my taking over, he would disengage, sometimes completely leaving the kitchen. Honestly, that sometimes felt like a relief. I was tired and hungry and I just wanted to eat. But Rett wouldn't learn that way. Getting too involved, by taking over, is a mistake I see parents making constantly, and from personal experience, I get why.

So Scott and I created some rules for ourselves. When Rett's cooking, we decided, one of us needs to be present to answer his questions. But we need to be doing something else, too—paying bills, reading an article, or doing some work—so we are not there exclusively to oversee Rett. We need to stay on the opposite side of the counter. That keeps us from getting into his space and stems the temptation to take over. We also need to suck it up if a meal isn't all that good or the kitchen is messy. We need to prioritize his learning and development and be willing to make ourselves a bit uncomfortable in order to foster it.

From Rett's point of view, his goal is to make dinner once a week. He has a plan—the recipe and the ingredients—and he implements that plan, asking questions of us as he needs to. He gets to show what he knows every time we eat a meal he's cooked. As for reflection, we have long had a system in our family where we put every recipe we've made in a plastic sheet to save, and we each "rate" it, from 1 to 10, and indicate what we liked about it and what we didn't. (I told you we were a little obsessed.) So we had a built-in mechanism for giving Rett feedback that is honest and actionable and for him to talk about what he learned and would do differently. As a result, slowly but surely, Rett is learning to be a capable cook. As parents it seems like a relatively small investment (one meal a week over a five-year period) to know our child will leave us prepared with the skills to eat healthfully. In a way, potentially eating cereal for dinner, in the case of a complete failure, is the easy part. The hard part is the work we need to do with ourselves to productively let go and trust the structured process of growth.

CHANGING ROLES

Watching our kids fail—even in small ways, like burning dinner—is challenging, but I think the struggle with self-direction is even deeper. The fact is, when kids are self-directed, the role of the parent changes. And it's not always clear what the new role looks like.

Early on a Saturday morning, the house was quiet. I'd been gone all week and arrived home well after everyone was asleep the night before. As I reached for my first cup of coffee, Scott came into the kitchen from walking the dog. He was visibly upset.

"What happened at the park?" I asked.

"I tried to help Rett with his math while you were gone and it was a nightmare," Scott stated matter-of-factly. "You guys don't have a textbook and so I couldn't figure out how he was supposed to solve his math problems because he does it differently than the way I know."

It took a moment, but I realized Scott wasn't talking to his wife and he wasn't upset about the dog park. He was talking to the leader of the network of schools his child attended. I shifted gears. "Can you tell me what happened?" I asked.

He took a deep breath and said, "Rett was studying for math this week and he asked me for help. I looked at the problems he was trying to solve and I couldn't remember exactly how to do them. I asked him, but he solves them in a different way than I was taught. So I asked him for his book, and he doesn't have one. I asked him for the instructions, but he doesn't have any. All he has is a playlist online."

I nodded and asked, "And then what happened?"

"We had to go through the playlist together and it took like twenty or thirty minutes."

"And?"

"And we figured out how to do it by using the resources on the playlist. And he was able to solve all the problems and we checked the answers, but one of them isn't right and I don't know why it isn't right or how to get that answer."

"Does it matter that he couldn't figure out that one problem with you? Can't he get help from his teacher on it?" I asked.

"Well, he didn't finish it," he said.

"But why does that matter? It sounds to me like you figured out the concept together and it took about thirty minutes. Isn't that what we want? For him to understand math?" I queried cautiously.

"But he didn't answer all of the problems correctly," he said, as if I was missing the obvious.

"Was he able to get help from his teacher and figure that last problem out?"

"Yes."

"So I don't understand the concern. He doesn't have to turn in those problems. He's not going to be graded on them. They're designed for him to learn the concept. If he understood and asked for help from his teacher and you, isn't that what we want him to be doing?" I asked, now genuinely puzzled.

"I didn't know how to help him," he explained. "I've always known how to help him. Usually I just quickly flip through the textbook, remember the way to do the math and then show him. I couldn't do that. We had to watch a video together to figure it out." I now heard a trace of fear in Scott's voice.

In that moment, a bunch of things started to make sense—not just about what was bothering Scott, but also about the worries I've seen in so many parents as they've encountered Summit. For the previous six years in elementary school, Scott knew and understood his job. I supported English, and he helped our son with math. He knew how to do that. It was familiar and comfortable, and suddenly, he didn't know how to do his job as a parent anymore.

The bottom line is: Scott and I, like all parents, like being needed by our child. As Rett began to access the tools and build the skills to direct his own learning, it completely changed our role. It felt uncomfortable that he knew more than we did. But it was the best way to prepare him, and in time, we would figure out our new place, too.

Chapter Six

Reflection: Max's Mentor

One research study after another shows that kids who have even one meaningful relationship with an adult in school have better outcomes than those who don't. But there's no system in place in schools to make this happen. In a typical fifteen-hundred-student high school, the caseload for a counselor is four or five hundred to *one*. I knew this all too well because I'd run a counseling department. Counselors had just two twenty-minute meetings per kid over a four-year period. They weren't mentors or advocates—they were data processors. That's all they could be. They couldn't possibly get to know every kid on their list. So when it came time for a student to apply for college, who knew her well enough to write her a letter of recommendation? Not her counselor, certainly. Maybe, if she was fortunate enough to have tested into AP English, she thought that teacher was a good pick—AP would look impressive to schools and presumably an English teacher would be a good writer, right? That's what everyone else thought, too, and so they'd all asked the AP English teacher to write their letters. These teachers, already burdened with the job of teaching, couldn't take on writing twenty, thirty, forty letters and so were compelled to set a limit. Or in the worst case, they said yes and then, pressed for time, carbon-copied letters, changing little other than the name of the student. I'd been confronted with the reality of this my first year as vice principal in Mountain View, when Stanford University denied admission to several of our students after receiving identical letters of recommendation for all of them. Their rationale was that if a teacher couldn't take the time to write an original letter, then the students must not have been compelling enough for admission. I could certainly appreciate Stanford's position, but I also understood the crushing load our teachers carried.

We wanted a different way. What would it take for students to be so well known by their teachers and mentors during their senior year that writing an original letter of recommendation would be obvious, even easy?

We started with the concept of the "homeroom" and decided to make it actually feel like home, like a safe place you could go for support and where you would be known. As a high school teacher, I'd learned kids were hungry for this. My classroom had always been occupied before school and at lunch by kids who didn't feel there was anywhere else safe to go. They'd sought refuge in the quiet calm of my room, but they'd also sought connection. They often wanted to help me, or to talk, to share detail of their lives. Really they wanted to be seen.

We landed on the creation of mentor groups as we opened Summit. We drew on a wealth of research that supports advisory programs, but purposefully chose to call our teachers mentors instead. Advisers give advice. Mentors are experienced, trusted guides. Each mentor has an individual relationship with each mentee, but they also lead a group that spends lots of time together. They are essentially the nuclear family for each student in the Summit community. We are very careful in selecting groups that are heterogeneous, balanced by gender, race, academic skill, and economic background. We want every group to be as close-knit as the "houses" of Hogwarts. While we stop just short of having a Sorting Hat ceremony, we do make getting welcomed into your mentor group a really big deal.

The mentor's role is to bring to life the values of the school, and get the kids to internalize and live them. The mentor groups meet regularly to talk through their goals and help one another solve problems. Each student also meets one-on-one with their mentor, weekly. That mentor knows each student's family. They do home visits and learn things like if the kid has a traditional Somali home with six brothers and sisters, and which older sister the mentor can talk to if the mom can't be reached or can't understand English well enough.

Most important, the mentors stay with the group year after year. The mentors, with just fifteen or twenty kids on their list, get to know the *whole* kid, meet them where they are, and help them achieve the goals they've set for themselves. There's no question of who will write the letter of recommendation.

WHEN SOMEONE BELIEVES IN YOU

We got to see the incredible impact of our mentorship program immediately. It started with what's come to be known as the Speaking Out project, which is now a rite of passage at Summit. Every kid who has been through the ninth grade with us has been a part of the exercise Adam and Kelly designed during our first year. Students are required to choose a subject they feel passionate about and to take a position. They exhaustively research it and write a paper. Then they work that paper into a speech they practice, practice, and practice, even—as in the case of Adam's class—doing so while navigating an obstacle course. Then they give it to a small group of peers, then to a larger and larger group until they've presented in front of their whole ninth-grade class—all the while, they've been collecting feedback and improving. The ninth-grade class selects six to eight speeches they feel are the best, and those students give their speech in front of the entire Summit student body and community. The Speaking Out project turns tradition on its head: it's not upperclassmen presenting to the younger grades but the other way around.

Max, a freshman with a really significant stutter, was in one of the first classes to do the Speaking Out project. The moment "speech" was mentioned, he panicked. He put everything he had into researching and writing, hoping Adam wouldn't require him to speak. While Adam wasn't Max's mentor, he was a mentor to many other Summit students and so, like all of our teachers, had begun to bring a mentoring mindset to his teaching. Adam maintained a calm, steady, and firm stance that Max would complete the entire assignment, and receive lots of support in doing so. So Max moved on to rehearsing, telling Adam each day just how bad it was. Max signed up for the last slot on the very last day to deliver his speech. It took Max five times longer than what had been allotted to him because his stutter made his pacing so slow. The class ended several minutes before he finished, but everyone stayed silent and in their seats. When Max was done his classmates gave him a standing ovation.

The class ranked Max's as one of the strongest speeches, meaning he would go on to give it in front of the whole school, which at this point was scheduled for the very next day. At first, Adam worried that their intentions in voting for his speech came from a place of teasing. He swung by my office to give me an update, saying, "My knee-jerk reaction was disappointment, because we have worked so hard to create a nice school culture, and here these kids were being mean to Max. They were trying to set him up to fail." But he had checked in with students individually, and they expressed with genuine enthusiasm that Max's speech was awesome. Adam had to agree. The effort Max had made to write an incredible speech, in hopes of not giving it, had paid off. It was objectively one of the best.

Max wasn't as sure, telling Adam that he didn't think he would come to school the next day. Adam pulled in Max's mentor, Angelica, and they sat with Max for several hours after school, talking it through and strategizing. Max reasoned that he had fulfilled the assignment. He had given the speech. What more did they want from him? Adam and Angelica asked Max to reflect on the experience of doing something he thought he couldn't do and hadn't intended to even try. He reluctantly admitted it felt really good to finish and to receive a standing ovation. He talked about how once he started giving his speech, he was so focused on getting through that he didn't think about much else. He wondered if there was a way he could do it better. Adam saw an opportunity and began asking Max what his next goal would be. Even though Adam wasn't Max's mentor, this is the beauty of the mentorship mindset, one I saw over and over again over the years as the team came together to support a student. Because teachers wear both hats—teacher and mentor—they let each role inform the other, making them stronger at both.

Adam and Angelica told him it was his choice, but said, "You know you're going to regret it if you don't show up tomorrow." Max wouldn't commit, but said he would think about it.

As far-fetched as it sounds, that night Max went online to learn about how to cure a stutter, and discovered one of the options was a machine that you could put in your ear. It was available at a community center that was about to close, but they were willing to stay open and wait for him to pick one up. Why no one had ever researched this machine before has remained a mystery. What we do know is that this was the first time Max had taken his stuttering into his own hands and looked for a support himself. He practiced the speech with the machine that night and got it down from twenty minutes to eight. He realized he was actually going to do it.

The next day the entire student body gathered to hear the speeches in the largest room we had. We called it "the dance room" because one entire wall was covered in floor-to-ceiling mirrors. We used to draw straws for who had to teach in there because it was really hard for a group of teenagers not to get distracted by their own images. But we'd learned to make the best of our first facility, as quirky and untraditional as it was. We were lucky to have it at all. The room was packed, with everyone sitting on the floor. An old podium covered in decades' worth of political bumper stickers stood at the front, ready for our speakers. Max's mom and dad had been on the phone throughout the night with Angelica. They experienced a kaleidoscope of emotions, bouncing back and forth between extreme protection and cautious optimism. They really had no idea what to do, and so ultimately had agreed to let Max decide. Max's dad—a huge bear of a man who worked as an electrician—stealthily came into the school that morning, and told us, "Max said I can't be here, but I need to be here." We set him up at the rear entrance of the room, believing he would be able to see Max without Max seeing him. Adam still remembers looking back just as Max finished his speech and seeing tears stream down his dad's face as the whole school gave his son a huge standing ovation.

Years later, Adam and Max reconnected. Max shared that giving the speech in front of the school that day remains a memorable moment he holds on to. It remains a moment I hold on to, too. I don't remember the topic of Max's speech, but I do remember the look of elation on his face when he finished. A look that only comes when a person has achieved something they never believed was possible, and suddenly their whole view of themselves has changed. I also hold on to it as an example of what happens when you know kids, when you have a personal relationship with them, and when you create a safe space so they can come to know one another and themselves.

THE POWER OF REFLECTION

A huge part of the mentor's role is to do what Adam and Angelica did with Max: to ask questions that provoke the mentee to reflect on what they want, who they are, what they care about, how they feel, and, ultimately, what they should do as a result—not because someone told them to do it, but because it is an authentic choice for them. It is during moments of reflection that learning and growth take place. As a school committed to mentoring and reflection in service to learning and growth, we thread the approach through everything we do.

Summit Prep's sophomore English class had been working on the Passion Project for weeks. The project's essential question was "How can you use your interests, curiosities, and passions to contribute to your community and better yourself?" Each student had picked a subject and gone deeply into researching it. An early step was pitching their project to their peers, since they were all going to be learning from one another as they went. Then they blogged about their process of researching and developing expertise on their topic. The final steps of the project were to write and deliver a TED Talk, showing their passion for what they'd learned and how they were applying it. In some ways it was a project similar to Speaking Out, by design. The ability for students to practice skills and habits over and over is critical; while the kids were practicing familiar skills, they had selected entirely new topics so the project felt fresh and interesting.

On the day I participated, they'd just begun to review the scoring guide they'd use to give feedback on one another's speech drafts. Ms. Hernandez provided a set of example essays ranging from mediocre to professional. The students' task was to give feedback by using the guide. They were commenting on the author's claims and use of evidence, among other key skills.

As a former English teacher, I'd given feedback on hundreds—if not thousands—of essays, and so I felt pretty at home. I asked if I could join a table, and the students handed me a scoring guide and the model essays. As we worked through the practice feedback round, it felt like I was working with a group of peers. The students were really good at giving specific, detailed, and accurate feedback. I looked for anything they might be missing, and came up short. The teacher asked them to post—in a shared folder the whole class could see instantly online—how they'd scored each essay, and for a member of the group to explain why. If there were discrepancies between different groups, the class discussed them until everyone was clear, then they moved to the next essay.

This class systematically calibrated the scoring guide. In a matter of thirty minutes, every student in the room was able to come within half a point of how the teacher (and I for that matter) would have scored the essays, and to give really specific feedback on how to revise. It was brilliant and powerful. I thought about how many full weekends I had spent grading essay after essay and trying to give as many useful comments as possible, only to have my students look at the grade, shove the paper in their notebook (or worse, the garbage), never to look at it again. All of the painstaking notes I had made were lost. When the students submitted their next essays, I would most often find the exact same mistakes. Later in my teaching, I held individual meetings with students, wherein I'd use a scoring guide and give feedback before they submitted the final draft. That was an improvement, but it still revolved around me as the teacher prompting the feedback and them mostly just doing what I'd told them to do.

In the Passion Project, the kids gave the feedback. They had really internalized the expectations, which made them far more open to receiving feedback because they understood it. Finally, this critique was all happening in the *early stages* of drafting, a time when students were most open to learning and growing as they worked toward a final product that would not only be viewed, but graded, by their peers. The process of thinking about other people's writing was a key part of improving students' own writing, and reinforcing their self-reflection. Over the next hour as I watched the students in that tenth-grade class, I found myself longing for the opportunity to teach again, just so I could handle feedback this way.

When I'd taught, my students had looked at the grade I'd

given them and processed the letter only. They'd think, *She gave me a B,* whereas this sophomore group could see the bigger picture: *My claim is at a 6 right now, but my evidence selection is a 5.* When I'd taught, my students would get their grade—good or bad—and know there was nothing they could do about it. The grade was the grade and it wasn't changing so they didn't have a lot of curiosity about my comments, why I'd pointed out the problems I had, or what they could do differently. It's a helpless feeling. I know, because I'd been in the same position as a student. This sophomore group, in contrast, was looking at the feedback they were getting and thinking hard about it. They were processing what they had seen in others' work and trying to figure out how to apply it to their own. They were given the space to do it and an incentive to keep working, which heightened their motivation. When I'd taught, my students felt the grade I'd given described *them.* But this sophomore class understood the score described only their level of performance on a specific skill at that particular time. If they didn't like it, they had the ability to change it.

Reflection happens in Summit classes each and every day, and is a critical part of learning and growing in all skills. It is a significant part of goal-setting, and holds a valued place in the self-directed learning cycle. The point of reflection is to inform the setting of the next goal, so there will be improvement and progress. In the case of this class, each had set a goal to develop a TED Talk. Some entered class that day with a full draft. Others had a partial draft and others, for a variety of reasons, did not have drafts. In every case, they were able to benefit from the calibration and feedback. For those without a draft, they had a better understanding of what was expected and where they were in relation to their peers, which helped them start writing. They also had the encouragement from the group to just do it, and some individual mentoring from their teacher during the session to help them figure out *why* they weren't executing their plan, and how to get unstuck.

Ms. Hernandez got the students to identify the outcome they wanted, the plan they'd made, and what was blocking them. She prompted them to consider their emotions and their behaviors and to put themselves in the shoes of others . . . including her. She asked questions like "Does this project impact anyone else besides you and in what ways?" For all, the answer was yes, but for different reasons. For one, his performance in school impacted his mother, whose dream was for her son to be educated and successful in a way she didn't think she was. For others, it impacted the subjects of their project, so that "Why Snowboarding Needs a New Olympic Sport" would help aspiring snowboarders worldwide, and "Moon Bears and Me" would help save the nearly extinct species. In each case, the student left the conversation knowing their goal and why it was important to them, as well as their specific plan for achieving it.

By missing the practice of reflection, the traditional grading model in America falls short. Looking back, the tools I used for kids who had missed assignments (scoring zeroes and Fs, taking points off for being late) weren't learning tools at all. My tools didn't help the student learn writing skills, because after all, how could I give feedback when they hadn't turned anything in? My tools didn't help to motivate them, because once the student was in a hole, it felt impossible to dig out; indeed, in many cases, it was. My tools didn't help with self-direction, because inevitably the student could blame me, or the assignment, or the timeline, because it was all about me giving them direction and them following, or not. The discussion was never about them owning their own learning. I never asked them to think about their learning process and make it better. I wasn't a mentor to them.

That evening, I reminded Rett to write a thank-you note to the mom of a friend who had taken him along on a ten-day trip. He was twelve and playing with his Legos, and clearly didn't want to leave them for this task. I'd hated writing thank-you notes as a kid, so I felt more than a little bit of sympathy as I said sternly, "Now. It will only take a few minutes. Gratitude is important." He sighed, but agreed, then showed me the letter before sealing the envelope:

Dear Leela,

   Thank you for taking me with you on Alex's Eagle Scout project trip. It was really fun.

Thank you,

RETT

Ugh. Though serviceable, it didn't really do justice to what he was capable of, or to how amazing the experience had been for him. I didn't want to fight with him—I wanted to have a productive conversation. But how? That question raced through my mind as I read the card over a few more times and turned to Rett. I had an idea, sparked by my time on the Passion Project that day.

"Hey, buddy, I appreciate that you sat down and wrote the card. I'm wondering, why are you sending Leela a card?"

"Because you told me to."

"Okay, I did ask you to write a thank-you note to Leela because she took you on a big trip you absolutely loved, but why else are you writing it?"

He paused for a moment to consider and then said, "Well, I really do appreciate Leela. She put up with all us boys and did a lot of work to make sure we had a good experience. And when I got sick she took care of me."

"Okay, well, do you think she knows that?" I asked.

"I said thank you at the airport," Rett said, then sheepishly added, "but we were really tired, so maybe not."

"And do you want her to know it?" I questioned.

"Well, yes."

"Okay, so the reason for writing a thank-you note is so Leela, someone who you appreciate, knows you're thankful for her and what she did for you. That seems worth a few minutes of your time, yes?" He nodded. "So the next question I have is, does the note you wrote actually convey to Leela the message you want to share?"

"Yes." His answer was quick and certain.

"Are you sure? Look at it again," I pressed him. He took the card. "Why don't you read it aloud to me?" With an eye roll, he did. Then I asked, "Aren't you guys working on making a claim and supporting it with evidence at school?" Rett attended Summit's middle school at the time.

"Yeah."

"Isn't this the same skill? Aren't you claiming to be thankful for Leela and that because of her efforts, you had an amazing experience?"

"Yeah," he responded again.

"Well, if you were using your scoring guide from school on the claim and evidence you used in this note, what would you give yourself?"

He took a deep breath and reluctantly said, "A two."

"And where are you working to score at school right now?"

"A five." He turned and walked away, saying, "I get your point. I'll rewrite it."

As he left the room I pumped my fist in the air. It wasn't every day I had a parenting moment that went that well. But it sure felt good when it did. If only I could stay calm, not get frustrated, and use some of the basic questioning tools we used every day at Summit, I could make much more progress as a mom.

ASKING THE RIGHT QUESTIONS

Mentor is a role we *should* be well equipped to play as parents. We hope that we are trusted by our kids. We spend years and years feeding, bathing, clothing, sheltering, nurturing, teaching, and playing with our children, all of which are actions designed to build trust. But occupying the role of mentor is easier said than done—we have so much of ourselves wrapped up in our kids, and therefore so much emotion surrounding them that meddles with our ability to take a step back.

Something I am constantly working on with Rett is my ability to set my emotion and myself aside, so I can simply be there for him. At my best I can listen, ask genuine questions, and help him to see his own logic and emotion in a situation. At my best I resist interrupting or judging him, and I let him come to conclusions and decisions that likely wouldn't have been possible without my presence, but aren't mine. There are a set of questions Summit mentors use all the time, and I try to remember them when parenting. They are open-ended questions, questions that beg for thoughtful answers:

> *What do you want from this situation?*
> *What emotions do you have?*
> *What behaviors are you exhibiting?*
> *What is working or not working? Why?*
> *Put yourself in the other person's shoes—what do you think their perspective is?*
> *What role can you play in getting to your desired outcome?*
> *Is there anything you need to do to make the relationship right?*

We ask reflective questions verbally, and we also ask them in written form—which is particularly useful when helping to mediate a conflict between two or more students.

On one such occasion, Justine sat forward in the conference room chair. Her left heel tapped rapidly and she pulled her hair taut in both hands. Her eyes were fixed on a pink sheet of paper resting on the table in front of her. She didn't move as I entered and made my way to the seat next to her. Since she was visibly agitated, I sat close enough for her to know I was there, but far enough away to give her some space, and waited. After a few minutes she turned to me. Her eyes were fiery and her voice defiant as she said, "I didn't do anything wrong."

I sat with my body language purposefully open, with both feet on the floor and my body turned to her. I spoke calmly and in a neutral tone. "I honestly don't know what happened. I'd like to understand. Why don't you write down your thoughts in response to the questions on the reflection sheet in front of you and then we can talk through it."

"I don't have a pen," she retorted.

"We can fix that," I said as I handed her one. In a room down the hall, Kelly was having a very similar conversation with Estelle.

Justine wrote for about ten minutes and then I prompted her to share her answer to the first question: Describe what happened.

She nearly spat the words at me. "Estelle was talking about me behind my back and I'm not going to stand for that kind of disrespect, so I told her I knew what she was doing and it better never happen again and she just started screaming at me."

"How do you feel right now?"

"I'm pis . . . *mad*."

"What else do you feel?" I pressed.

"Disrespected."

"What's the feeling under that?"

"What do you mean? It's disrespected," she said.

"Yes, and that makes you feel hurt? Vulnerable? Frustrated? Or maybe something else?" She paused for a moment. Her eyes dropped, and she said, "She's supposed to be my friend. Friends don't talk bad about each other." I gave her an encouraging look. She kept going. "I'm mad at her for doing that. I . . . now I . . . I can't trust her."

"And how does that make you feel?"

"Like I can't be her friend."

"It looks like that might make you sad." She slowly nodded. I held her gaze for a minute and then turned to the pink sheet. "Can you describe what happened from Estelle's perspective?" Justine had written the word "same" under the question. It took about ten minutes of back-and-forth, but we finally got to a place where Justine acknowledged she had only "heard" Estelle was talking about her and when confronted, Estelle had denied it.

The next question was "What was your role in the situation?" It pushed Justine to further consider how her unwillingness to even listen to Estelle and the aggressive way she approached and confronted her helped lead to the screaming match that ensued.

Now calmer, and starting to think clearly about the circumstances, Justine wondered out loud what Estelle had to say. Reluctantly she admitted it was possible Estelle hadn't talked about her. She even reflected that it would feel terrible to be accused of something you didn't do.

Together we practiced what she wanted Estelle to know and what she could do to repair the situation. A few minutes later we were sitting with Estelle, who had been doing the same work and walking through the conversation with

Kelly. With prompting and support from Kelly and me, the girls talked through their answers to the questions. They needed the sentence starters and the notes they had taken to keep them from devolving into anger and shouting again, but as the conversation progressed and they actually listened to each other, they did the hard work of repairing the rupture in their relationship.

In most schools, when two kids get into a screaming match, either no adult notices or, if they do, the kids are disciplined, perhaps suspended for a day. Unfortunately, punishment doesn't actually address the relationship problem. It's common for videos of fights to end up on social media where they fester and grow into multi-student feuds and often violent encounters. It is human to disagree, to become angry, to get hurt, and to hurt others. It is healthy to learn how to repair relationship ruptures, so they don't escalate to a point of no return, but instead relationships become stronger from the process of healing the break. Like many kids, I didn't learn how to repair relationships from my parents. And so I found myself learning side by side with the kids at Summit.

The pink reflection sheets capture the basic science behind relationship repair with questions prompting each party to put themselves in the shoes of the other, get in touch with their emotions, clearly articulate the facts, and to look for the role they can play in a solution. But the sheet is only a tool. Without a mentor to support and guide, to ask questions and hold up a mirror so reflection can take place, growth is unlikely to occur. The work is time intensive and draining. Most people don't like conflict and would rather avoid it or move past it as quickly as possible. And so, especially in big schools, it becomes easier to just avoid people than to engage them. Until it's not.

Equipping kids to develop and maintain healthy relationships is not traditionally the domain of schools, and so taking it on requires the school to make a commitment. Schools have to create a community where every relationship matters. If everyone doesn't believe relationship skills are part of being prepared for adulthood and the structures aren't in place to allow time and follow-through, it simply doesn't work. But when a school commits to mentoring and reflection, there are benefits that extend beyond the development of interpersonal skills and the ability for kids to feel safe. The same reflective process is what helps kids to begin to understand themselves, who they are, and ultimately to have a sense of self.

"INGS" VERSUS CAREERS AND MAJORS

I observed a recent one-to-one tutoring session with a student named David. He had just finished an internship experience for what we call Expeditions, or periods throughout the year where a student gets to do a deep dive into an area of interest. David was an eleventh grader who had spent a previous Expedition learning software coding and was sufficiently interested to explore it more deeply via an internship at a local large technology company. For his most recent

Expedition, he embedded with the company's engineering team. On the day I observed, David and his mentor were coming together to reflect on the experience.

"What was your goal for the internship?" the mentor, Mr. Lee, asked.

"Well, I'm trying to figure out what I want to study in college. Coders make a lot of money, so I wanted to try coding to see if that is something I might want to do."

"Tell me about the parts of the internship experience that went well, and why."

"I loved being at a company," David said. "It was amazing. I mean, they have free food, free snacks, they have great technology, you can get free haircuts, and there's a gym and a volleyball court."

"Okay," said Mr. Lee with a grin, "so you like the amenities of a tech company. Is that it or was there something more?"

"Well, yeah, they were great, but it was more about being respected. I mean, they just trusted, even us, the interns, to know what we needed to do and get it done and they made sure we weren't distracted and had everything we needed to get our work done. I liked feeling respected, you know, like a professional, where I could make my own decisions."

"Great. What else went well?"

"I really liked the team meetings. Especially how they would always start with a problem and then everyone would work to solve it. The issues were really interesting and most of the time I didn't realize there was a way to solve the problem. It was pretty amazing to hear the creative ideas people had. Some of them were terrible, but then there would be a good one."

"Okay, so what are the 'ings' of what you liked about those meetings? For example, I think I heard you say you like the part where you were solving problems."

"Yeah, solving problems, and I like brainstorming, it felt really creative. I liked how we worked together and bounced ideas off of each other."

"So, problem solving and working with others on brainstorming or creative thinking. What didn't go as well?"

"The coding!" David sighed deeply.

"Oh, well, okay then. Tell me about that."

"I hate sitting at a computer for hours and working by myself. I know I'm not that good yet, but even as I get better, I still can't imagine doing that all the time. Some of the engineers I met—well, most of them, actually—love it. It's their favorite time."

"That's helpful. So what specifically don't you like about it?"

"I don't like working alone for long periods of time. I don't like how you do all of this work and if you get one tiny thing wrong it doesn't work. It was so frustrating."

"So I hear you learned you don't like working alone for long periods of time, and work that requires absolute precision can feel frustrating."

"Yeah. But I learned about this other role that isn't an engineer. It's a product manager. They work with the engineers and most of them know basic coding, but as far as I can tell, their job is to help figure out what problems the technology is trying to solve for real people and translate that into something that can actually be built. They were in all of our meetings and I got to talk with some of them."

It was a huge win that David learned his feelings about coding after six weeks of exploration in high school, rather than midway through an expensive education where he majored in it. Still, many would view this internship as a bust. David didn't figure out what he wanted to major in or the career he wanted to pursue. If he had gotten the standard question, "Do you want to be an engineer?" his answer would have been "no," and something even more important may have been missed.

"What do you want to do?" "What career do you want?" "What do you want to major in?" These are common questions that lead to a common result: kids will find an answer to latch on to and stick with—"doctor," "lawyer," "teacher," or whatever. That could have easily happened here, but instead David and his mentor used a version of reflection to dig underneath the job and into what could be learned about David from the experience.

By asking him to focus on his "ings," his mentor was helping David to figure out all of the little interests that are unique to him that ultimately add up to who he is and what he cares about, which can lead him to understanding the type of work that will be purposeful and meaningful to him.

One of the most effective shifts I've made with Rett has come from what I've learned in mentoring. I never ask, "What do you want to be?" or "What is your favorite subject?" Rather, I ask, "What do you like doing?" "What parts of that do you like most?" And in the course of our conversation we come up with a list of what we call the "ing" words. In experience after experience, he has accumulated more and more "ings" and is beginning to see a pattern. So now, when he thinks about his future, we aren't searching for a specific degree program that leads to a specific job; instead we are talking about a variety of things that matter to him and how he could find all of them reflected in something specific he wants to do next. That gives me confidence in a world that is rapidly changing and where the careers of today will supposedly be gone tomorrow. Because Rett knows what he is looking for in the form of "ings" and is building valuable habits and skills, I'm sure there is a match for him, even if it hasn't been invented yet.

Collaboration:
Leave No Husky Behind

I love so many of the activities we lead during student orientation, but the balloon activity is my favorite. This year I was partnered with Mr. Rodriguez to facilitate. We had pushed the tables to the edges, allowing for a big open space in the middle that was filled with a mountain of blue balloons. As the students entered, we handed each a brand-new, super-sharp No. 2 pencil and told them to grab a balloon. Even for newly minted high school freshmen, the combination of sharp pencils and balloons was irresistible, so Mr. Rodriguez got right to it. "Let's circle up. We're going to play a game. If your balloon survives the next minute, you get a prize. Go!" The room erupted into chaos as kids ran around popping one another's balloons. Laughter, shrieks, and loud pops filled the air. Some kids hid under tables while others

jumped on top of them. Even those who initially seemed re-
luctant quickly started to pop others' balloons, while trying
to protect their own. I called time.

"Let's come back together and talk about what happened,"
I said.

As the kids formed a circle, they looked around, searching
for a surviving balloon, a winner. As the emotion, adrenaline,
and excitement of the last minute settled, a few faces looked
confused.

"No one won. Everyone's balloon is popped," said a girl,
with a hint of disappointment. She'd spent the minute under
the table, trying to protect her balloon, only to have it popped
during a sneak attack from the side.

"If no one has a balloon, maybe the winner can be the
person who popped the most balloons," offered a particularly
aggressive boy, who had indeed popped a lot of balloons.

"Yeah, I got seven of them," offered another boy. A few
others began to share their self-recorded scores.

"We never said you had to pop anyone's balloon to win,"
said Mr. Rodriguez calmly.

"What? That makes no sense," said a boy, Jimmy, whom
I'd already spent some time talking with the previous day.

"If no one popped anyone else's balloon," Jimmy pressed,
"then who would win?"

"Everyone," said Mr. Rodriguez. He let it sink in for a few
minutes. The muttering in the room signaled a collective
mental processing. I could see the students trying to imagine
a scenario where everyone could win . . . and struggling
with it.

Mr. Rodriguez asked everyone to sit and the two of us

started to describe our school, how we were a community filled with individuals with different long-term goals and paths, and different skills and needs. We explained how success would look different for each one of us, and didn't have to come at the cost of anyone else. Each of us could be successful and we could help one another succeed as well.

ALL MEANS ALL

Every family who enrolled a child at Summit had spoken either to me or to a member of our team. In those conversations, no parent ever said to us, "It's okay if my child doesn't make it to graduation or college or into a good life. Don't worry. Someone's got to fail. It's fine if it's my kid." In fact, in my nearly three decades of being an educator, I've never heard a single parent willingly give permission to a school to fail their child. I had looked every parent in the eye and promised to prepare *their* child, not a percentage of our students or some portion of them, but their individual child. This was a fundamentally different compact with parents from any school I'd ever worked in, or most schools in America for that matter. To live up to our promise, we were going to have to create a fundamentally different school, not just in how we educated our students and what we prepared them to do, but in our culture.

Summit had to be a school where we expected every single student to succeed, a school where every child would discover who they were and what they wanted. Every Summit graduate would leave ready for college, ready for a career, and ready to live a good life, on their terms. By definition, Summit couldn't be a school where there were winners and losers. We couldn't run a traditional high school where college prep classes were rationed for a few and kids were stack-ranked by GPA so that those at the top benefited at the expense of all those below. If we were to have any chance of preparing all our kids in all of the areas they needed, they would have to be learning every minute of every day, and not just from their teacher, but one another. So we had to form a culture where they worked together, supported one another, and viewed one another as teammates.

The balloon activity showed what we were up against. Most students' instinct, whether by nature or nurture, was to compete in order to succeed. If we didn't intervene and show them a different way, both in school and in class, we would fail them, and I would break the promises I'd made.

COLLABORATION: THE COMPETITIVE ADVANTAGE

The benefit of creating a collaborative versus competitive school culture extended well beyond preparing each and every individual student. A majority of the founding Summit parents were professionals and employers. They had a first-hand view of the skills they looked for in hiring and had a hard time finding in employees. They knew from experience that the skills employers want—from complex problem solving, to coordinating with others, to emotional intelligence— are enhanced by, or require, working well with others. These weren't just Silicon Valley skills. Wise and successful businesses across industries marked collaborative cultures and approaches as a competitive advantage, and study after study confirmed their position. One such study showed how teams outperform individual decision-makers 66 percent of the time. And when they made the team more diverse, if it included different ages, genders, and geographic locations, that percentage rose to 87 percent.[1]

But collaboration doesn't happen naturally in the workplace or school. Our schools and businesses are saddled with a culture that is by definition competitive. Schools were designed to sort and sift kids to determine which ones were best at a small number of valued skills so they could be funneled into different life opportunities. When the system came into being, the different paths carried with them different life prospects and outcomes, but each offered the potential for a fulfilling life. Not so today, when the difference between being a high school dropout, high school graduate, and college graduate translates fairly cleanly to a life of poverty versus economic security, with the gap widening daily.

Like most others, I was brought up in a culture of competition, which was never more apparent than when I was in the tenth grade and my English teacher led our class through a simulation based on the Prisoner's Dilemma. In the simulation, every member of a group stands to be imprisoned for some length of time. It is clear to each member of the group that if everyone sticks together they will all be imprisoned, but the length of their sentence will be much shorter than if they turn against one another, in which case those who remained loyal would receive lengthy sentences and the one who turned first would receive no time. Like all good simulations, many lessons and dilemmas surfaced, including trust, collaboration, fairness, and the welfare of the individual versus the group. As I played through the rounds with my high school peers, I remember being completely shocked as time and time again, they turned against me and one another in an effort to "save" themselves. While many started out with the inclination to collaborate, it quickly disappeared as they received longer and longer sentences, while others got off free, at least for that round. In the end, every one of us ended up in jail for a very long sentence. I remember being deeply disturbed that we hadn't been "smart enough" to stick together. Instead we'd let the skillful and well-trained simulation facilitator tear us apart.

While not as dramatic as a prison sentence, I had experienced the same dynamics in school and as a professional. I had been raised to compete and had oftentimes—due to some combination of hard work, determination, privilege, and luck—succeeded. But at what cost and at whose expense?

During my interview process with Summit, a successful business leader said to me, "China has more honor students than the U.S. has students." I don't know if the statistic is true, but the concept stuck with me. I'd already grasped that no parent was willing to sacrifice their child so someone else's could be successful, but hadn't thought about it in terms of what our competitive process meant globally. To compete internationally with a country that vastly outnumbered us, could we actually afford to sacrifice any of our kids? Given our relative size, didn't we need every American to compete?

CONSENSUS VERSUS MAJORITY RULE

When I accepted the role of Summit's founding principal, I was going to be an employer for the first time in my life. I was going to lead a team to build a school from scratch, which meant if it wasn't the school I believed in or valued there was no one to blame but myself. As I shared this sentiment at one of my first board meetings, one of the members wisely said to me, "A culture will develop in the organization. The only question is, will it be the one you want?" I was deeply fortunate to have the support of many knowledgeable and thoughtful leaders who had incredible insights and many tools for building teams and organizations. I admit that in the moment, devoting time to learning from them felt pretty luxurious. I was worried about finding a physical building, hiring, and recruiting. I had a narrative in my head that if I didn't get teachers and couldn't make payroll we wouldn't even have a school, so I could worry about how to build our team later, when I actually had one. I couldn't have been more wrong. Thankfully, Summit's board understood the value of focusing on creating the right organization from day one and continually pressed me to dedicate a portion of my time and energy in this direction.

We started with consensus. One of the frustrations I had experienced time and time again while teaching was the drawback of majority rule, our natural way of doing things in America. The problem with majority rule is that whoever loses doesn't have an incentive to buy in to the direction of the majority. In fact, the loser is often incented to sabotage. I saw this play out over and over at Hawthorne or Mountain View when a decision would be made, say, to adopt a new textbook or focus on a particular goal, but a good portion of the teachers would say, "I didn't vote for that," close their classroom door, and do what they wanted to do. It is so common in education that there's a phrase to describe the phenomenon: "This too shall pass, so I'll wait it out."

The best decisions are those achieved with a full consensus. That doesn't mean everyone will get exactly what they want—often no one will—and it doesn't mean everyone will be equally happy with a decision. However, done right, consensus means everyone agrees to support the decision and they are held accountable by the group.

Summit's first faculty was a team of seven. Compared with most public-school faculties in America (76 percent women and 80 percent white) we were diverse, with four women and three men, spanning in age from early twenties into late forties, and including four whites, one Latino, one Asian, and one mixed race. Diversity was intentional when we had just those seven teachers, and it's remained so now that we have over two hundred and fifty. Not only do diverse teams make better decisions, but experience with diverse people prepares kids for work and life in our rapidly changing society.

Many years later this would be affirmed time and time again as Summit's graduates reported about their experiences in college. One of the big advantages all of our students felt they had was four years of practice building relationships and friendships with people who weren't like them. They observed how many of their college peers struggled. Often this was the first time they'd spent time with someone who was so different and it came at a high-stakes moment, when they were trying to navigate living together in a 250-square-foot room. By contrast, Summit's graduates had spent years in close proximity to people from all different backgrounds and felt comfortable navigating the complexity that such a dynamic brings to relationships.

FORMING, STORMING, NORMING, AND PERFORMING

During the summer of 2003, our differences didn't seem to matter. The Summit staff was in the first phase of developing as a team, what psychologist Bruce Tuckman calls the "forming" stage. All of us had taken a huge leap of faith to start a school we deeply believed in and the optimism and opportunity were palpable. Plus there was so much work to be done and it was so much fun to do it with other people, rather than alone, which is what we had all experienced in our previous teaching and leading roles. There were a few moments when someone would say something that rubbed another the wrong way, but we were all being polite and so we just pushed those moments aside and continued forward. And then the kids showed up and it got really hard, really fast. That's when we entered the second phase as a team: "storming."

It was the second week of school. As a team we met two to four hours a day and yet it wasn't enough time to make all of the decisions we had to make to get a brand-new school going. Because we were aiming for a fundamentally different outcome (helping all kids succeed), and therefore a fundamentally different culture (collaborative versus competitive), we couldn't afford to simply transport systems and ways of doing things from our previous experience into our new school. Rather, every single thing, from how we served lunch to how we calculated grades, had to be designed to match our values and drive toward our desired goals.

None of us were sleeping very much and all of us were engaged all day long in an effort to establish relationships and expectations as quickly as we could with our students. It was emotionally exhausting work and we were all a bit stressed. Five minutes past the time that our meeting was supposed to begin, everyone sat at the conference table except Adam. He was late again. Kelly was visibly agitated. "He's always late," she remarked under her breath just as Adam entered the room. Sensing this could mushroom into something more, I reminded Adam of one of our core values, respect, and that arriving on time and ending on time was one way to show respect. He earnestly turned to the group and said, "I'm sorry. There's just so much to do, I don't have a minute to waste, so I make sure everyone is ready to go in the meeting before I come in."

I thought Kelly might explode. "So I'm supposed to waste my time sitting here getting ready for you to enter, so you don't waste your time? How is that fair?" At the time I didn't understand the phases a team will go through to get to a productive and collaborative rhythm. If I had, I would have felt more comfortable with the discomfort, or storming, and led productively through it. Instead, I said the first thing that popped into my mind to try to lighten the moment. "This reminds me of *Fast Times at Ridgemont High,* when Jeff Spicoli's teacher says he's wasting his time and Spicoli says, 'If *I'm* here and *you're* here, doesn't that make this *our* time?'" No one laughed. We didn't need stupid movie lines, we needed real tools to work together.

With the help of some experts, Kelly, Adam, the rest of the team, and I came together to learn and implement some basic tools in the third stage of teams formation, "norming." We created a booklet of shared expectations so we could work together more effectively, and "start on time, end on time" was not only an item in the book, it became a mantra, ultimately one of the expectations of our culture that persists to this day.

We also created a simple but powerful decision grid. It's easy to come to consensus when everyone is going along to get along, but without a structure for efficient decision-making, the second there's disagreement it falls apart. Our decision grid clearly and transparently communicated who had the authority to make which decisions (D), who could veto a decision (V), who could make a proposal for a decision (P), and who could simply give input (I). We wanted to make important decisions by consensus, but we also were prag-matic about the sheer number of decisions we had to make each day. So we agreed that our expectation was, the decider for each decision would seek to gain consensus, but if it

Sample Decision Grid

This grid can be useful for documenting who is in each role for a set of decisions.

	Stakeholder #1	Stakeholder #2	Stakeholder #3	Stakeholder #4
Decision A	Role	Role	Role	Role
Decision B	Role	Role	Role	Role

Role Codes

D / Decision: Person or people who make the decision

P / Proposal: Person or people who are involved in developing the proposal

I / Input: Person or people who provide input on the proposal

V / Veto: Person or people who can veto the decision

MBI / Must Be Informed: Person or people who must be informed of the decision

---

wasn't possible in a timely fashion or because folks just couldn't agree, the person with the D next to their name decided and everyone would support the decision.

This simple shift changed the dynamic of our group dramatically. If someone felt strongly about an issue but wasn't the "D," he was incentivized to articulate a compelling position in order to bring folks together, but it made no sense to be intransigent because it wasn't his call anyway. Further, even if a person was the D, if he didn't seek consensus on his decision, others weren't incented to invite him into other decisions.

We also learned quickly that no one wanted to make all of the decisions, but everyone wanted to know who would decide, how decisions were made, and what role they played in them. It was one of the more valuable and interesting insights I had. I always assumed everyone would want the power to make all decisions, but that proved not to be true with both faculty and students. Rather, they want to make the most important decisions to them and they just want to know how to engage on all of the others. It took some work and commitment to get through this norming phase, but the decision grids we built and the simple tools we used became so invaluable, we still use them today.

By the fall we had entered the fourth and final phase, "performing," which meant we were working well as a team. Some groups will move quickly through these four phases, others will slow or even stall out. Some will loop back and take a circuitous path, but in the end they will all go through all four. Just knowing the phases makes a huge difference, especially when the group moves from the polite, introductory state of "forming" into the more turbulent "storming" phase. Groups who are prepared for the coming storm, and view it as a productive stage to getting to a more aligned, "norming" place, fare better. Those who don't know it's natural to storm often fall apart in this moment, declaring the group a failure. We realized our kids needed the same skills we were building, if they were going to be able to collaborate and work together. We decided to simply teach them what we were learning.

LEAVE NO HUSKY BEHIND

I will admit it can be terrifying to cede control to kids. I love teenagers, but the truth of the matter is their brains are still forming and so biologically speaking they are still developing the neural connections required to make good decisions. But if we really wanted to teach them to collaborate, we had to give them real and meaningful decisions to make.

To get our first school opened, my team and I had already made decisions about many things the kids were interested in, such as the name of the school and the school colors. But on our opening day, we didn't have a mascot. This presented a big opportunity, as the kids cared deeply about the mascot. The teachers and I let the students know, as the inaugural Summit Prep class, they would get to choose. We explained our decision-making grid, and how they, as a group, were the "D." We emphasized it was a big responsibility. This would be the mascot for every Summit Prep student from then on, so they had to look at whatever decision they made with future generations in mind. They also needed to choose a mascot that reflected our school identity. Finally, we explained the difference between making decisions by consensus versus majority rule. The choice for the mascot, we explained, would need to be a consensus. Every single student would have to give a "thumbs-up" in order to move forward. If someone gave a "thumbs-down," that was their right, but then they would also have to make a suggestion to make the proposal better. We, as the faculty, would be the "V"—though we certainly would not want to veto a decision they made by consensus, we could. So it was in everyone's best interest for them to engage us in the process, too.

We took it slowly. In addition to our decision-making grid, the faculty also had a simple and powerful approach to decision-making and problem solving we called the *STP*, and that, too, we taught to the kids. It started by *forming the problem they were trying to solve into a question.* In their case, "How can we choose a mascot for Summit that will represent who we are today and in the future?"

The next step is to *identify the status* (the S), which required gathering facts and opinions from everyone, without judging or editing. This step was key. It involved everyone and surfaced the different experiences kids had had with mascots, so they would have a handle on where they were starting from. The diversity of thought was amazing. For some of the kids, their school mascot had been a huge source of pride and identity. They had clothes and cheers and it made them feel a part of something. For others, their experience had been totally different. They didn't see themselves in their mascots and didn't understand why they were supposed to feel loyal or connected to a symbol that didn't resonate with them and, in some cases, even offended them. Many had never thought about a mascot. Others became really curious about the history of mascots and a few discovered just how controversial a mascot can be. Most took the responsibility for naming it for future students very seriously.

The next step is to *define the ultimate target* (the T). We call it the magic wand step. If you could wave a magic wand and get the perfect answer to the original question, what would it be? At first kids thought the target was the actual mascot, so we helped them realize the target was the criteria for an optimal solution. In other words, it was how they would know that they'd come up with an idea that fully answered their problem statement question. The criteria were things like: It shows people who we are and what we all care about. It has qualities we aspire to have and exhibit. It is timeless. It can be represented in a drawing or symbol.

Finally, they *develop proposals* (the P) for how to get from the status to the target. They were working on making argumentative claims in class, so we brought that into the work they were doing to persuade their classmates. At our monthly all-school meetings, groups had formed organically and would present their mascot proposal. They made their case and got feedback, then adjusted their proposal for the next meeting. One group proposed the mascot be the Samurai Squirrel. Their classmates, who quickly realized they could use the criteria from the target to question a proposal, grilled them:

"What does that mean?"

"That's not a real thing."

"Imagine kids coming here in ten years. How would the Samurai Squirrel make sense to them?"

The Squirrel supporters made their case, but couldn't build momentum for their cause. One student named Danielle was particularly passionate about the Samurai Squirrel, but her enthusiasm wasn't catching. Another group made a case for becoming the Summit Prep Trojans. Again, they were grilled:

"How is that representative of who we are?"

"What does that say about what we want to be?"

"Um . . . weren't Trojans kind of violent?"

A month or so in, a group came to me and asked for my help. They really wanted a school pet, and so wanted to come up with a mascot that would also work as a pet. I told them a live animal was not going to join our Summit family, but suggested it was an interesting place to start brainstorming. What kind of pet or animal would be representative of who we were as a school?

The group researched extensively, then came back to me with the Husky. Huskies are pack animals, and their loyalty and courage were representative of our core characteristics. They had also learned that huskies are playful. "They're just like us, Ms. Tavenner." They put together a compelling presentation they planned to give to their classmates. I suspected they secretly hoped if they succeeded I might give in and let them get a husky puppy.

Before they were ready to present, though, they needed to take another step: they needed to build a coalition. They knew other kids, like Danielle, were passionate about other ideas. They had to seek out the Squirrels and the Trojans, listen to their interests, and try to incorporate their ideas and wants into the Husky proposal. That way, everyone would see their needs represented.

Were there themes the Trojan people cared about that were also true of the Husky? The Trojan group was mostly athletes and they wanted a mascot that could be fierce and a team player. Together they figured out that, as sled dogs, huskies all worked together, pulling in the same direction to reach their goals through the cold and snow . . . which was perfect given we were Summit. Someone had read *The Call of the Wild* and relayed that huskies could be quite ferocious and were also majestic, intelligent dogs. The Trojans were in.

The Squirrel contingent wanted a cute mascot. The Husky group figured out a husky could be both a puppy and a grown dog. After all, what's cuter than a puppy? So Team Husky revised their mascot drawings to include puppy versions. Someone even found a cuddly stuffed animal husky.

They made their proposal at the next schoolwide assembly, working in elements from all of the coalition-building they'd done, and making a case for how the Husky was representative of Summit because the Husky would never leave its pack. As the balloon exercise had emphasized from the very first week of school, they were coming around to the idea of never leaving their fellow Huskies behind, and they would be stronger together rather than pitted against one another. Together, they would all reach the Summit. They reached consensus, and we became the Summit Prep Huskies.

WHEN COLLABORATION GOES BAD

Just as we worked on collaboration on a schoolwide level, we also worked on it in the classroom. It was challenging during that first semester as teachers, kids, and parents alike carried baggage from their history with group projects. In fact, I've noticed the fastest way to ignite a round of nightmare school stories among parents is by mentioning a group project. The frustrations and complaints are common, and legitimate.

"The other kids in my child's group didn't do anything."

"My son had to do all of the work and they all got the same credit."

Or the reverse, "There was a really bossy kid in the group and my child couldn't get her ideas heard or accepted."

"She didn't feel included or valued and the group did something she wasn't proud of."

"My child didn't learn anything."

"They could never agree, find time to meet, or divide the work evenly and so they got a bad grade and my daughter suffered."

While many parents become agitated, complaining to teachers and principals about the unfairness of group work, others are more resigned. "Well, welcome to the real world," they may tell their kid. "That's what it's like working in teams." We need to do better and be explicit about how to work in teams, and teach collaboration as a valuable skill, not just a means to an end.

Group work goes wrong in two primary ways. First, most often the task assigned isn't actually worthy of group work. What groups do well is solve complex problems that benefit from different experience, expertise, skills, and knowledge. Groups aren't better at completing tasks that are rote or linear, with a single right answer. When kids are put into a group and asked to complete a worksheet or find the answer to a math problem that requires a discrete skill or piece of

knowledge, inevitably one of the kids will be best at that particular thing and won't need the others to produce the best
work. Typically, everyone in the group knows this, and so
when they simply let the "smartest" kid do the work for them
all, they're acting rationally. The second way group work
goes wrong is when the task is sufficiently complex, but no
adult is teaching and supporting the skills required to work
collaboratively.

Ms. Chan had pulled up a chair to sit with Group Three.
A few days into the Probability project, they were stuck. Not
on the actual work, but as a group. It was a math project with
real-world implications. They were working with exponents,
but ultimately they were figuring out the impact of interest
and borrowing money. These ideas were going to come into
play countless times in their lives and most certainly in a few
years as they considered financial aid packages for college.
But the group wasn't functioning and so a few minutes earlier Kaylen had asked Ms. Chan if she and Marco could form
their own group. The answer was no, but came with support
from Ms. Chan.

Ms. Chan began, "So it sounds like the question before us
is how can Group Three work together to productively finish
the Probability project. Is that correct?"

"Are you saying we aren't going to be able to break into
two groups?" Kaylen asked.

"That is what I'm saying. Part of what we're learning is
how to work with different people and how to collaborate. If
we just stop working together when things get hard, we
won't learn those skills," she said. Kaylen didn't object and

the others nodded. This wasn't the first time at Summit they had been asked to work to repair and strengthen relationships with others when they weren't getting along.

"So let's start with the status," Ms. Chan said. Over the next several minutes all of the group members described the facts and their opinions about what was going on. A pretty common story started to emerge from the various perspectives. John was an excellent math student. He had always been an excellent math student, and probability was really easy for him. The other members of the group weren't as strong at math, but they brought some other interesting strengths to the project. Marco, for instance, had been working with his dad in his landscaping business for many years and as a result had some firsthand experience with banking, loans, and the real-life implications of money. Kaylen and Lidia had both worked to save money for big purchases and so they knew something about interest. Everyone in the group knew what they knew, but none of them felt the others valued what they brought. They all struggled to speak honestly and openly with one another about their feelings. Their reticence had led them to treat one another in ways that didn't feel good or productive. Now they just wanted to get away from one another.

Once Ms. Chan helped the group start to talk and listen to one another, she was able to step back a bit. She suggested they set group goals for what they wanted to accomplish together and then devise a plan to get there that allowed each of them to bring their unique strengths. They were back on track, but over the next week Ms. Chan would check in many times, sharing feedback and observations, as well as encouragement and coaching. In the end, they were able to accomplish the goals they set for themselves and learn the value of staying engaged in a relationship, even when it was difficult.

COLLABORATION AT HOME

As we got better and better at teaching collaboration skills at Summit, I recognized how applicable it was at home, too. My family collaborated—or tried to—every time we had to make a decision or solve a problem, whether it was how Rett would get home on a day neither Scott nor I could pick him up, or how to make sure our dog got enough exercise. In other words, it comes up almost every single day. For most families, gone are the days when every member has a separate and distinct role that doesn't overlap with another. The complexity of life today means everyone must pitch in and work together. In our family, my work requires me to be on-site in schools and often traveling around the country. Scott works from a home office. A traditional approach to the division of tasks like grocery shopping, cooking, cleaning, car maintenance, bill paying, and school pickup and drop-offs would be impossible for us. We've got to collaborate, not only with one another, but with friends, family, and neighbors if we have any hope of accomplishing everything we want. Most families work together—the question is, does the experience help to develop valuable skills our kids need to be prepared for life?

On the nice-to-have end of the spectrum, friends of ours use family vacation as an opportunity for their family of five to collaborate. The mom and dad felt frustrated after they spent a lot of money on a nice vacation no one enjoyed, and everyone complained about. They wanted to approach vacation planning differently, so they issued a challenge to the whole family: "We have one week of vacation. Our budget is this amount. Where should we go and what should we do?"

At first, everyone was ecstatic. Ideas immediately began flowing, but what they quickly realized was, everyone had a different trip in mind. The youngest wanted to go to Disneyland, while the eldest wanted to go camping. It wasn't long before frustration and anger bubbled up.

Fortunately, this family employed some basic tools, using the STP process—"identify the status," "define the target," and "develop the proposal"—that we used with the mascot selection, the same tool we use all the time at Summit. In the end, not only did they end up with a vacation that was on budget, but every family member felt invested in the itinerary. When they got to parts of the trip that weren't their first choice, they knew it was important to someone they loved and why, and they focused on enjoying being together or having a new experience, as opposed to just doing what they wanted to do. And they knew that what they really wanted was coming and others would engage in it even though it hadn't necessarily been their first choice.

WHEN IT ALL COMES TOGETHER

In the same way navigating a car to a destination requires a combination of left and right turns, stops and yields, so does creating a pathway to preparedness for our kids. Collaboration requires real-world opportunities, and also self-direction, because you cannot be an effective collaborator if you're not self-directed. Collaboration and self-direction, in turn, each require self-awareness. The most successful collaborators know themselves. They know who they are, what they care about, what they know, and what they don't know. Knowing themselves comes from being reflective. Successful collaborators know their strengths and what they are working to improve, and they know what they can contribute. They can work with their classmates to pick a mascot, their friends to pick a movie, and their family to plan a trip or even choose a pet. And when they grow up, I'd hire them for my team any day.

PART III

WHAT

IS PREPARED?

'**ve been asking myself the same three questions every day**
since I started Summit.

- Is Summit the school I wish I had attended?
- Is Summit the school where I would want to teach?
- Is Summit the school I want to send my own child to?

If the answer isn't yes to all three questions, something is
wrong. It's the simplest and most honest way I know to ensure
the schools we run are good enough for everyone else's children.
But the answers aren't measurable by anything but my gut, and
so they don't serve as very good indicators for anyone else.

Habits of success, *curiosity-driven knowledge*, *universal skills*,
and *concrete next steps* are the measurable outcomes that mat-

ter most if we want our kids to be prepared for a good life. They are the destination we program into our GPS, and how we know if a student is prepared to enter adulthood, succeed in college, and pursue the life they want to lead. *This* is where we're going.

Chapter Eight

Successful Habits:
The Building Blocks

Kelly Garcia remembers the conversation taking place in her classroom, but in my mental movie we stood in front of the bathrooms outside of room two. That's the only discrepancy in our recounting of what became, for each of us, one of the most profound and impactful moments in our careers as educators, and in our journeys as moms. With the perspective of sixteen years, it's easy to look back and point to this exact moment as a turning point, but I think even then we both had a sense of the significance.

It was late October during our first year at Summit. Kelly had asked to speak to me about one of our ninth graders, Zack. She wanted to let me know Zack was going to fail her class, and she felt it was important we notify his family. She proposed we mail "progress reports" home, as the schools she'd taught in for the previous seven years always had.

As the first semester had unfolded, our team of seven took turns catching one another when we proposed enacting a system before thinking through if it actually fit the Summit culture. We'd committed to deeply analyze if it would move us toward or away from fulfilling the promises we'd made to our families. It seemed clear to me Kelly was tired and frustrated in this moment, and so it was going to be my turn to ask the hard questions.

"How is it possible Zack can fail your class in November?"

She was quick with a very clear answer. "He isn't productive in class. He refuses to put pen to paper—and it's clear he doesn't do anything at home." He literally hadn't completed one homework assignment the entire year, she explained, and no one on the home front was particularly supportive. His situation was all the more aggravating because he was skilled in many areas. When Kelly got into debates with him, his chain of thought was logical and well expressed; in technical terms, he was great at "argumentative claim." But he couldn't pass history by making great verbal arguments about why he wasn't doing his homework. Mathematically he was so far in the hole he wouldn't be able to dig his way out, even if he completely changed the next day. "He's not doing anything he needs to do," she finished.

Kelly was seeing Zack as one of the two hundred kids she had taught at her previous school. As an overloaded teacher, what could she do but look at the evidence in front of her— Zack wasn't making any effort whatsoever—and then respond to that evidence by bubbling in an F? Maybe it would teach him a lesson, but most important, it would clear some space so she could focus on the other kids who could possibly make it. This train of thought was not only common in every school we'd ever worked in, but completely understandable: *I've done what I need to do, and you haven't. I'm going to wash my hands of responsibility now.*

"Have you really done everything you can do?" I asked her. "If you're honest with yourself, have you? Have we? Are we going to be just like every other school? Are we going to be the school that bubbles in the F and takes no responsibility for what we know will come next?"

"I'm sure I haven't done *everything* I could possibly do, but he hasn't done *anything*," she responded with exaggerated enunciation.

As I asked Kelly the questions, I was also asking them of myself. We both understood what would happen if we gave Zack an F. He would not graduate. He would likely not get his GED. He would struggle to make a living, and he would turn to doing what he could to get by. He would probably end up doing something dangerous and/or illegal, and eventually end up in jail, or dead. It sounds extreme, but we'd both seen it play out so many times with kids just like Zack. It was possible that even if Kelly failed him, he would have an experience, a mentor, or a breakthrough that would wake him up. But statistically speaking, he was more likely to stay on a downward spiral. What's more, I had guaranteed Zack's mom that her son would graduate prepared. Even though she wasn't doing much at home to support him, I couldn't get that promise out of my mind.

"Are you telling me you are ready to give a fourteen-year-old kid the death sentence?"

I could see from the look on Kelly's face the emotional blow my words landed, and I could feel them in the pit of my stomach, but I couldn't stop. "Have we done every single thing humanly possible to change the trajectory of his life? We promised we would." It wasn't that I thought we could—or should—"save" Zack. Summit wasn't about riding in on some majestic horse and swooping kids up into a better future. But Kelly knew, and I knew, we could give him the tools to have the life he told us he wanted.

Later Kelly told me that part of her wanted to scream, "Enough! I'm tired!" She had her own family, she needed to sleep and stay sane and keep part of herself for herself. How could we ask her, or any educator, to do more? We couldn't. It wouldn't be the right answer anyway. We didn't see ourselves as saviors. Even if she had enough to give to Zack, she'd be completely burned out for the next Zack, or the one after that. A one-off approach would make teachers crazy, and teachers pushing themselves to the point of burnout does not make for sustainability. I was pretty intense in those days, but even I was reasonable enough to see that.

I will be forever grateful that Kelly didn't yell at me in that moment. She also didn't walk away or quit. She had every right to do any of the three. Instead she recommitted and agreed to go back to the drawing board with me to figure out a path forward.

This conversation and the ones that closely followed shaped the direction of our school. It's a direction we've built on for the last sixteen years, and continue to improve to this day. Kelly made a list of everything she could do to support Zack, but every item involved her doing something *for* him and involved *her* time. This was problematic for three reasons: If there were too many kids like Zack, there simply wouldn't be enough time in the day, even if we were willing to not have any other life. Second, it wouldn't develop Zack. What happened when his next teacher didn't do all of those things? Finally, I couldn't help but remember that I had never wanted anyone to save me, I just wanted people to make it possible for me to save myself. Maybe Zack felt the same way.

So teachers doing more couldn't be our answer. Instead we had to figure out how to enable kids to do for themselves. It turns out that meant we needed to value developing the habits of success as much as we valued developing academic skills and knowledge.

THE BUILDING BLOCKS

Zack was just the first in a long line of kids who caused Summit to take very seriously the responsibility to teach and help our students develop habits of success. Our commitment to the success of every single student took us deep into the science and research to understand what habits matter most to truly prepare our kids for their future, and also to ensure their success today.

The framework we've used in our pursuit is the *Building Blocks for Learning*, which was developed by Dr. Brooke Stafford-Brizard for Turnaround for Children,[1] and pulls together decades of the best research in education and learning science. The framework identifies sixteen specific skills, all of which impact school and life success, and all of which can be developed and improved. They typically develop progressively, with more complex skills building upon earlier, more basic ones. The Building Blocks for Learning has been the most useful single tool we have found, mostly because it helped to streamline and simplify a vast amount of information and knowledge into a pretty simple graphic we could wrap our minds around.

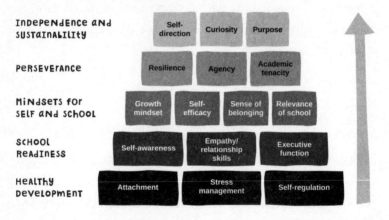

BUILDiNG BLOCKS for LearNiNG

InDepeNdeNce aNd SUSTaiNabiLity	Self-direction	Curiosity	Purpose	
PerSEVErANce	Resilience	Agency	Academic tenacity	
MiNdSeTS for SELf aNd SchOOL	Growth mindset	Self-efficacy	Sense of belonging	Relevance of school
SChOOL ReAdiNESS	Self-awareness	Empathy/relationship skills	Executive function	
HeALThy DeveLOpMEnt	Attachment	Stress management	Self-regulation	

Looking at the building blocks as if we were living in an ideal world, the "base" level of the pyramid involves healthy development that would begin in early childhood—attachment, stress management, and self-regulation. As those become solid, the child moves toward what one might think of as school readiness habits: being self-aware; having some relationship skills; and strong executive-thinking habits, such as planning and goal-setting. Building on that, the child develops strong habits in the way to think about himself and about school, which includes adopting a growth mindset, self-efficacy, a sense of belonging, and an acknowledgment that school matters. At the penultimate level of the building blocks, the focus is perseverance. At this level the child is able to recognize his relevance to the world around him, has a sense of agency or autonomy, and makes it a habit to push through challenges in his academic life. Which brings us to the top level of the blocks. This is the trio of habits that all the rest have built up to: self-direction, curiosity, and a sense of purpose. Kids who are prepared enter adulthood having demonstrated they can transfer these three habits from one setting to another, from school to work to family to community, without support.

The world we live in is not ideal, however, and at Summit we often encounter kids who have not successfully developed earlier building block habits. In Zack's case he didn't feel he belonged in an academic environment and struggled to understand the relevance of school, as a result of a complex web of experiences and messages in his life. Other students had never formed an attachment before, or had never developed the habit of self-awareness. We often don't immediately recognize which block a kid is missing—we just know the structure supporting a student's learning is rickety. As a faculty, we use the habits of success building blocks to guide us as we look for the underlying issue.

When we abandoned the idea of failing Zack, we turned

to figuring out why he wasn't doing any work. As we began to understand his underdeveloped sense of belonging, the first thing we did was double down on him. No matter how much he tried to give up on us, we made clear we would never give up on him. We all started sending him messages in every form we could think of that we wanted him to be at Summit because we believed in him and his capabilities and we were going to stick by him. By doing so, we disconfirmed everything Zack not only expected, but that he was waiting for. He wanted his teachers to bubble in the F so he could just go play video games. That was the easier, familiar path. But we collectively wrapped our arms around him instead, and it worked. Though it wasn't easy, and at some moments it was messy, he did graduate from Summit. The rejoinders to Zack were consistent, insistent, and relentless. They weren't yet systematic, but we would get there.

We know, based on a breadth of research, that these sixteen *habits of success* are used again and again in life. These are the power habits—the ones that will help us succeed in school and beyond. We also know they are interconnected. For instance, consider self-direction. Summit students regularly practice the self-directed cycle. What might not be obvious is how executive functions (goal-setting and planning) are intrinsic to this process. So as kids practice their self-direction, they are both drawing from and strengthening their executive-function building block. The building block of a growth mindset, or the belief your talents can be developed, is also critical to the self-directed cycle. When those students reflect at the end of an hour, day, week, or semester, they strengthen the habit of growth mindset. Certainly, not all kids have these habits when they begin practicing the cycle, but with consistent feedback, practice, and reflection, they develop them over time.

At the top level of the building blocks, a student can take the habits he's formed and apply them in multiple contexts— not just in school—and without support. So imagine a kid who practiced setting a goal, making a plan, executing it, showing what he knew, and reflecting (the self-directed cycle) a ton of times over his life, in school or at home. When he gets a summer job at the local grocery store—restocking shelves, collecting emptied carts, and bagging groceries—out of sheer habit, he uses a similar process to guide his work. He walks into the store each day and recognizes what needs to happen even before his boss tells him what to do. He sets goals for how quickly and efficiently he can collect the carts and devises strategies to do it better each time. He embraces the challenge of making sure every customer's groceries are packed in a way that nothing gets smashed, they can lift every bag, and they are ready to go by the time the transaction is completed. Contrast that to the kid who is found leaning on counters or lounging around every time he doesn't have a specific order from a manager. Which kid would you hire? Which kid are you trying to raise?

HOMEWORK JAIL

Over the years, we have built system after system at Summit to support the development of the sixteen habits of success in every student. During Zack's time we created a Mandatory

Academic Study Hall (MASH) in our first attempt to carve out a specific time and place for kids to practice and learn executive functioning skills and academic tenacity, as well as self-regulation and stress management. When the kids started calling MASH "homework jail," we had the feedback we needed to know our approach required revision. Iteration after iteration we looked at the research and science, talked to the experts, consulted our data, and designed the next best version of what we were doing. We'd then gather feedback and data, reflect, and do it all again.

Indeed Summit has evolved dramatically over the years. Today, the idea of homework has given way to simply the learning each student needs to do in order to develop and master the skills and knowledge they need. It doesn't much matter *where* it's done. Self-directed learning time is designed to build and support the habits Zack and others were missing, and creating an overall better approach to teaching and learning has made a huge difference. We have consistently pushed ourselves as educators to more clearly define what it is kids need to really know to be prepared and all the ways they might arrive there. This has enabled us to help students in ways that empower and make sense to them. If only I had done the same for my own child much sooner.

LABOR OR LEARNING?

Rett was in the fifth grade and I felt frustrated and angry after we'd argued over whether he'd done his homework. I was about to write my feelings in my daily journal when I glanced at the entries from the previous two years on the exact same day in October. To my surprise and dismay, they were the same sentences I was about to write. Was this *Groundhog Day?* Was I stuck in a movie where every year on the same day I was having the same fight with my child? Clearly whatever approach I'd taken with Rett didn't help, because here I was again, doing it all over, three years in a row. I started thumbing through the journal and was shocked to see the pattern take shape. Our homework argument wasn't a once-a-year thing. It was a pretty regular occurrence and, at least according to my journal, it left me in the same state of frustration and worry every single time.

What was I doing? There had to be a better way. My anger gave way to guilt and sadness. The next thing I knew, I was in Rett's room, hugging him and asking if we could please find a way to never do this again. Tired, and probably a little overwhelmed by my emotion, he agreed, hugged me, and sank into an embrace that was so filled with love I was sure my heart was going to burst open. It felt good and right in the moment, but I wasn't sure how either of us was going to live up to the agreement we'd just made.

I had tried everything to mitigate the homework problem. We had reward and consequence systems, special homework time and special homework help, a planner he had selected to record assignments, and a backup system in case he forgot. I had regular communication with his teacher and a disciplined routine of checking in. None of it seemed to work, and in fact the more systems I put in place, the more behaviors Rett seemed to develop to slip out of doing homework. Ironically, it was those avoidance behaviors that concerned me the most. Specifically, when he lied to me, whether it be about not having homework or having already completed it.

Grasping for a new approach to break open our impasse, I decided to try a strategy we used at Summit. When we had a student who wasn't completing work or was regularly off-task or disruptive, the first thing we did was to dig deeper. So I asked Rett *why* he wasn't doing his homework. I know it sounds crazy, but asking why wasn't something I frequently did, and if I did, I only asked once. This time, every time he gave me an answer, I asked why again. It was hard not to insert my opinions and dispute his facts, but after a bit, we got into a flow. Just like with the kids at Summit, the answer he gave to the first why and the answers he began to give after the fourth, fifth, and sixth whys were very different. The latter answers were much more insightful, honest, and, ultimately, useful.

When I first asked why Rett didn't do his homework, he said he did. It took all my restraint not to react to what I thought was another lie, and instead to ask why he thought that. He explained he did do his homework, either at home or at school during recess and lunch because he wasn't allowed to play until he finished it. It wasn't the answer I expected. In my mind, doing your homework after it was due or because an adult was literally standing over you and not letting you do anything else was not "doing your homework." But I maintained my curiosity and kept asking why. By the end of our conversation, I realized Rett's teacher and I had no idea what motivated Rett or how he'd understood the situation. As a result, the things we'd been doing had the opposite effect of what we wanted. We had created a completely unproductive context for everyone. Perhaps more important, the conversation made me wonder: What was our ultimate goal?

What I got from my conversation with Rett was that he didn't understand the value of the work he was being asked to do, especially since it was done during the times of the day he believed were supposed to be *his* times. Recess and after-school time at home were supposed to be reserved for him to play, be with his friends and his family. He understood school time to be time to do work and learn what the teacher wanted him to learn, but when schoolwork crowded into the time he deeply valued, it felt unfair. The situation was further complicated by the fact that he had no idea why he was being asked to do the homework in the first place. He didn't see the purpose of it, and as such he wasn't motivated to do it. Homework also caused problems in his relationships with both me and his teacher—fortunately two people he actually liked—which made the situation even worse. As it turned out, the only reason he did the homework was to try to preserve his relationships with us, but the cost was high as he was growing to hate schoolwork. As the cycle repeated, he'd also begun to think he wasn't a good student.

Obviously, as a ten-year-old Rett wasn't able to share this full analysis as I have, but I was surprised by how clear it was to me as I listened. The biggest problem was, I had never really asked.

I had to dig in more deeply. I started by thinking about homework. Why did I think it was so important Rett do his homework every day? In our conversation he had questioned the value of the work he was asked to do and so I looked at the assignments with fresh eyes. We'd been revamping homework for years at Summit and I think I had forgotten what traditional homework really entailed. He had a point. Most of what he was assigned was pretty rote. Step one: He was required to copy the assignments from the board and into his planner, so he would know what he had to do. He found this to be woefully inefficient and painful, but it was the required first step of completing homework. It was expected, checked, and graded. I had to ask myself, why? What is the purpose? What is the skill? What is the habit? It certainly wasn't a habit of success. In this day and age, with so many different possibilities for how to track responsibilities, assignments, action items, and appointments, why would we assume everyone would use the exact same process? Like with GPS, shouldn't we just define the outcome and then help kids figure out the best way for them to get where they are going? In this case, the outcome seemed to be completing the homework, but when I looked closely at the homework itself, I struggled to see its value.

The assignments, like the necessity of writing them down, were very directive. Rett was told to: read information and respond to questions about it; solve a set of similar math problems using a procedure; and practice writing words over and over in a second language. One assignment was to look up definitions for words in a dictionary, make flash cards, and memorize them. There were not choices or options and it didn't matter if he already knew the words. Completed homework was marked with a check. His teacher marked the math problems as right or wrong, and gave class quizzes on the word lists, but offered no other feedback on the work.

Rett didn't get his completed assignments back until days or weeks after submission. What was the purpose of doing all this work?

In a really humbling turn of events, I had to ask myself that question. Sure, I felt, what Summit teachers were doing today was significantly better than this, but I'd been a teacher for many years. I assigned homework to all of my students. I wrote the assignment on the board and asked them to copy it into their notebooks. I spent valuable time collecting, checking, and recording completion. Like Rett's teacher, I didn't give feedback—how could I? I barely had time to collect, check, and record. As a teacher, I'd noticed patterns. Some kids always did the work. Some did it neatly, some did it completely, most did enough to get by, and plenty didn't do it at all. Some copied it from others and many did it right before class started. Teachers are so accustomed to unsatisfactory homework completion that on our report cards we could select from several stock comments about homework behavior. And, of course, homework completion was factored into the students' course grade. For the life of me, I couldn't figure out why I had run a homework system like this for so many years. Sadly, my best explanation came down to this: good teachers give homework, good students do homework, and parents think that homework means something is being taught. Or so we all believe.

This exact same experience played out as Scott and I discussed the concept of chores for Rett. It would be easy to make a list of the chores we expected Rett to do and the way we expected them to be done, but what would he really be learning? Was our ultimate goal to teach him how to make a bed perfectly, or was it something deeper—teaching him how to navigate living in a shared space with others? And if the latter, why would I focus on a well-made bed? Parents often assign kids tasks, like setting the table, something that comes with rigid standards ("Napkin on the left under the fork, knives on the right, then plates, then glasses"); but rarely do we ask our kids to do things like figure out how to plant a vegetable garden in our yard, how to organize the space in the mudroom that is so messy no one can find what they are looking for, or even how to plan for a summer of no school with two working parents. I'm not suggesting parents do away with the more prescriptive tasks that simply need to get done, but we so rarely stop to ask what it is we really want our kids to learn.

STRONG FOUNDATIONS

Like most parents, Scott and I had an intuition about what habits would lead to life success. It came from our own experiences (good and bad) and our beliefs about what has made us successful and held us back. We've also read books and articles, each seeking to advance a particular skill, quality, or characteristic most important to future success. And of course, we talk to other parents about what habits matter. My friends and I have been told to raise kids with grit, and help nurture a growth mindset. We should want kids to be intrinsically motivated, and to have a sense of autonomy, all within a frame of positive discipline. We are privy to an overwhelming amount of information and an extreme mixture of opinions, and it's enough to make anyone crazy. My work at Summit, though, has enabled us to take all of the noise and advice and look at it through a compact—if sometimes academic-colored—lens.

What we want—and what most parents want—is to know that when my son reaches adulthood, he has all of the habits of success he needs to be on his own and live the life he wants to live. What I've learned as an educator is the top three building blocks are that destination, and he can't reach them if his foundation is shaky. And at the end of the day, if Rett is self-directed, curious, and has a sense of purpose—in multiple settings, and without support—I'll know he is prepared.

Chapter Nine

Curiosity-Driven Knowledge:
The Tutoring Bar

n 2012, we began to really amp up the ability for our high school students to self-direct how they would obtain knowledge—by which I mean facts, or, in the words of many educators, "content." We wanted to give them freedom and choice in the resources they accessed. For example, we didn't assign them a textbook chapter to read. Instead, for the hour per day that was devoted to their self-directed learning time, we gave them a whole playlist of resources they could choose from that included reading, video, podcasts, online simulations, and practice questions. We also gave them responsibility and tools for knowing when they had learned something, by choosing when to be tested on it. In short, students no longer took the same exact test on a specified day; rather, each student took it when he felt he was ready, and if he didn't succeed in demonstrating mastery of the knowledge, he had to keep learning until he did.

Early on, our approach to knowledge took some getting used to, but we quickly began to see the benefits of students directing their own learning—both in their development of habits, and in their interest in the subject matter. Each week, we surveyed each student about what was working and not working for them and why, and used it to make immediate improvements to their experience. For instance, they trusted one another to rate the quality of resources and wanted a way to show it, in the way that people review restaurants on Yelp or books on Goodreads. They wanted the resources organized by subtopic and a clear understanding of what they were expected to learn. They wanted more opportunities to practice problems and be able to see how they did.

Week after week, my team and I improved the resources, the environment, and the variety of choices offered. We discovered that while the kids were responsible for building a common set of knowledge they would all need to effectively engage with the problems and questions in their projects, they went about learning it in very different ways. It turned out, the kids were as curious about how to learn as they were about areas of interest for them.

The student feedback showed us kids felt respected when we gave them the choice of how to learn. We also noticed they started developing unique and personal ways to decide what to learn, when, and how. Some kids tackled the content of the subjects they dreaded first because they liked ending with the subjects they preferred. One kid compared his approach to that of a disciplined eater. He said, "I tell myself I have to eat my vegetables first because they're good for me. Then I can eat dessert." Others decided to race through and show mastery of an entire subject. This gave them a sense of confidence and accomplishment that helped them as they then tackled more-challenging subjects. And others took a very balanced approach. They would rotate through subjects, doing an even amount of each every week.

Student after student shared with us the process they were developing to figure out if they already knew something, when they knew something well enough they had mastered it, and how they determined the best way to learn something. They were all running little tests for themselves, as one student put it, "to learn how to learn."

As you can probably imagine, kids controlling their learning in this way was a radical departure from how content is normally taught and assessed. But in 2012, there was one thing we hadn't changed: conventional wisdom had prevented us from removing the requirement that every student attend a "class" on each topic and learn directly from the teacher. They had choice about all of the other ways and times to learn, but not that one. It was required.

Most people of a certain age remember Robin Williams in *Dead Poets Society* jumping on top of his desk and captivating his students day in and day out in his role as the "sage on the stage." Taken in contrast to Ben Stein's portrait of a teacher in *Ferris Bueller's Day Off* ("Anyone . . . Anyone?"), we have a very clear picture of what a good teacher looks like, and what a bad teacher looks like. A good teacher inspires, captivates, and gets kids to think by sharing profound knowledge and perfectly crafted questions. A bad teacher is boring and so the information she presents seems irrelevant and meaningless. However, in both cases, the teacher presents knowledge for the consumption of the students. The message to the teacher is: "To be good at your job, present knowledge—just do it in an entertaining and captivating way." It's hard to change a teacher's mind about their role, and it's hard to change a student's mind about the teacher's role. We learned both firsthand.

THE TUTORING BAR

At one point in the middle of the year, we noticed that for several weeks in a row when we asked students to rank which learning resources most helped them master the knowledge area they were working on, the mandatory teacher sessions scored dead last. At first, we dismissed the data, figuring that teenagers didn't like anything they *had* to do, especially once they had been given a taste of freedom. But as the results persisted, we agreed it wasn't professional or honest to ignore them. Someone suggested we test our hypothesis about their lack of enthusiasm—what if the sessions weren't mandatory, but optional? Would the kids then rank the teacher sessions higher? Everyone was worried. If they weren't mandatory, kids might not attend, and we felt their learning would suffer. Would we be committing the equivalent of educational malpractice? Finally, reluctantly, we all agreed to test it, but for one week only. We reasoned that if our fears came true and kids lost a week of learning, we could collectively make it up.

The result was not what we anticipated. Every student still attended the teacher lesson, and still ranked the experience at the bottom. What? We decided to extend the test for another week. Same result. And a third week, same result. Our kids weren't "losing learning" as we had worried, but they also didn't think the learning we were giving them was helpful. We were confounded. We used focus groups to try to figure out what was going on (if in doubt, "just ask the kids"). We brought a group together around this topic and the students told us they didn't believe the classes were optional. They were all afraid they would be marked absent or penalized for not attending. They were so conditioned by their schooling experiences that even when we told them they had choice they didn't believe it. So, in week four, we made *very* clear the classes were optional, like all of the other learning resources, assuring them in specific terms that they would not be penalized if they didn't attend. That week, class attendance lowered, but the bottom ranking stayed the same. For the next two weeks, fewer and fewer students attended the classes, but the rankings didn't move. Finally, in week seven, the class rankings shot up to the top spot! We couldn't believe it. But when we looked at the data we felt deflated; only two or three kids had attended each class. What was going on?

Each of these kids had ranked it as their top learning resource. Why? We asked each student separately, and yet they gave consistent answers: Previously, when they'd attended the class with lots of students, their teacher covered some ground they already knew well. Most of them had specific questions or were stuck on something they *didn't* know. They had to patiently sit through a bunch of stuff they didn't need to get to the small part they did. For some kids who struggled just to get started, the lesson had gone over their heads. They didn't feel like they'd gotten anything out of the time. We'd had a Goldilocks situation: Papa Bear's chair was too big, and Mama Bear's chair was too soft. But in week seven they had found Baby Bear's chair. According to the students, when only two or three of them showed up, the teacher set the preplanned lesson aside and asked the students what help they needed. Essentially, the teacher tutored the students. The time spent was shorter than the entire class period, and the kids felt like they got exactly what they needed, at the exact right moment, hence the reason for the very high scores. They all said there wasn't another resource that understood them and could support them in a way their teacher could.

The teachers, who had been growing very uncomfortable over the last many weeks because of their low ratings, reported a high degree of satisfaction as well. They felt like the session allowed them to really understand what their students were challenged by and then leverage their knowledge and expertise to support the student in a meaningful and efficient way. Even so, the teachers weren't fully convinced the teacher lesson should be optional. It was really hard to let go of the part of their job that everyone believed *was* their job.

So, we compromised. We agreed to another one-week test of what we called the *tutoring bar*, shamelessly modeled after the Apple Genius Bar. During self-directed learning time, we set up a tall table with a sign for each teacher that said "Tutoring Bar Open." Instead of offering a lesson, the teachers offered themselves and waited to see what happened. It didn't take long for the first student to approach the teacher for help, and then a second, and a third. The scores for the tutoring bar were our highest ranking that week, but we had one problem. Before we knew it, the line was really long and then the scores went down because of the wait. Then, organically, kids started helping one another while they waited in line. Pretty soon the bar was crowded with pairs of students helping each other in addition to the teacher helping. And suddenly peer tutoring was our highest-ranking resource.

Today, we have learning environments designed for teacher-to-student and peer-to-peer collaboration, and a technology platform allowing students who have demonstrated mastery in a particular knowledge area to share their willingness to tutor. The win-win is undeniable. Evidence clearly shows that when a person teaches someone else something, they gain greater mastery.[1] Leveraging students to appropriately support one another builds not only knowledge, but so many of the habits of success. And usually kids volunteer to be a resource about topics they're interested in. Their natural curiosity is transferred as they engage with their peers—in the same way that when I recommend a book I've just read, someone browsing might just decide to buy it.

The teacher role does not disappear with the new approach to knowledge. But it is different. Teachers are still everywhere in the classroom, whether during self-directed learning time or in projects, guiding, teaching, and supporting. The difference is, they focus their energy on high-impact, high-value interactions with their students. A Summit English teacher might lead her mentorship group through a "peel the cultural onion" exercise in the morning, lead a Socratic seminar during the Speaking Out project, and tutor a small group of students during self-directed learning time. They are no less critical than ever—their talents are just used more strategically. And students, for their part, don't become solitary figures disappearing into their laptops. They take what they've learned and apply it to the real-world projects they're working on alongside their team of classmates.

CAN'T WE JUST GOOGLE IT?

"Hey, Alexa, what are the official rules for Monopoly?"

It was Christmas Day and I was setting up the game with my niece Brooke. I had forgotten how much money each player starts with and she was new to the game. Our well-used version seemed to be missing the instruction sheet. At some point, it might have occurred to me to Google the information, but for the moment I was searching through the disorganized game cupboard for the paper sheet when nine-year-old Brooke queried Alexa without a second thought. Her first question didn't get us the answer, but after a few tries, Brooke casually announced, "Auntie Di, everyone gets six twenties."

Given the tech savvy of even elementary schoolers (not that asking Alexa a question requires tech skill, exactly), it's logical to wonder, should we even be teaching knowledge anymore? Between Alexa and Google, can't we get every answer we need, faster than we could recall it even if it did live somewhere in our memory? Why bother to learn things like historical dates, definitions of words, formulas, and grammar rules? Most of us spent a significant portion of our school years committing such information to memory, proving we knew it on tests, and then forgetting it soon thereafter. Do our kids need to do the same thing today? The answer is no. But knowledge still matters, a lot, and so they need to do something different.

LEARNING TO LEARN

The science of learning has consistently shown a correlation between kids' familiarity with a subject and their performance and skill. For instance, in one study, middle schoolers took a reading comprehension test wherein they read a passage about baseball. Those who had background knowledge about baseball scored higher, regardless of whether they'd been considered poor or good readers beforehand.[2] What this and other studies like it tell us is, if we want our kids to be good at valuable skills like critical thinking, they need to know and understand the stuff they are critically thinking *about*.

These study results resonate with our personal experiences, too. Most of us can remember a time we tried to read something yet didn't know a large number of the words. This can happen for young kids as they learn to read, but it can also happen to adult readers. For example, if I try to read a complex medical or legal text, I'll struggle to understand much of anything. Sure, I can use strategies like looking up words, and trying to figure out meaning through context, but the reality is if there are too many words I don't know, describing things I have no concept of, those strategies won't work. Even if I'm rapidly searching for definitions from Google, I can't hold all of the new information in my head long enough to make it through a sentence. I wouldn't be able to understand what I was reading. However, you could give me a similarly complex text on something I know really well, like education policy, and I could use those same strategies and figure it out. In one case I would look really dumb and in the other I would look really smart. I'm not unique.

This is where we have a really big chicken-and-egg problem. On the one hand, it's easier to learn more and perform academically when you already have knowledge about a subject, but the best way to acquire that knowledge is to learn about it. School makes this unproductive cycle even worse. Up through third grade, schools focus on teaching kids to read. However, in fourth grade, a switch occurs and kids are expected to read in order to learn new information. This obviously creates a problem for kids who haven't really learned to read by fourth grade, but as studies show, reading proficiency is heavily dependent upon how much you already know about what you're reading.[3] There are many implications in this for schools, but as a parent, my biggest takeaway is this: my child will learn more and perform better in school if he has a lot of knowledge to begin with.

A common temptation, unfortunately, is to try to cram as much information in our kids' heads as we possibly can. Parents often have this impulse, which is why we enroll our kids in places like Kumon and encourage memorization of facts by buying games that claim they will teach our kids important things. Teachers have this impulse, too, in large part because of a long-held societal view of the role of the teacher as someone who stands before a class, doling out knowledge. But there's another, better way for kids to acquire knowledge, one that stems from their innate curiosity.

The top three blocks in the habits of success are self-direction, curiosity, and sense of purpose. This is because as we think about adolescents moving into adulthood, we shift responsibility to them for their own learning and growth. Learning begins with curiosity. When a person genuinely has a question, the next logical thing to do is to seek an answer to it. People ask questions about things that interest them and generally aren't curious about things that don't. And outside a formal classroom experience, when someone wants to find an answer, they need to self-direct to get it. The solution to the chicken-and-egg problem, then, is *curiosity-driven knowledge*. Simply put, when we enable kids to follow their curiosities and interests, they learn much more. As they learn much more, they get better at learning. It becomes a virtuous cycle.

A PASSION FOR ROLLER COASTERS

Brody, a family friend who is a high school student, loves roller coasters. Plenty of teenagers love roller coasters, but he is passionate not just about riding them, but building models of them and knowing just about everything there is to know about how they work. His latest model stands over six feet tall and is an exact replica of a famous coaster in

Cedar Point, Ohio. It all started when Brody was over at a friend's house, and this friend had a K'NEX model kit of a roller coaster that Brody really liked. He asked for one for his birthday, and then assembled it with a lot of help from his parents. That led to another set and pretty soon his mom was searching for used sets because he built them fast, and they were expensive. His dad suggested they actually *ride* a coaster, and soon Brody was begging to go to the amusement park every weekend. Pretty soon he was consuming YouTube videos to learn all there was to learn about coasters. When he talks about them he sounds like a cross between an elated kid and a professional roller coaster engineer. What he knows about the construction, safety, design, and history of roller coasters makes him sound like an expert to any normal person, but his extensive knowledge is coupled with a true, almost palpable, joy.

If you think about it, you probably know kids like Brody— ten-year-olds who have a strong command of statistics, thanks to an obsession with fantasy football; or twelve-year-olds who can code because of their love for Minecraft. Brody was eight when he first became interested in roller coasters. If we were to catalogue all of the academic words and concepts Brody knows as a result of all of his roller coaster engagement, we'd see multiple subjects (physics, engineering, math, architecture, design, policy, and history), and his knowledge about them ranges from early elementary school concepts (basic gravity) through professional ones (acceleration and friction). His age and academic skills did not limit the development of his knowledge, because he accessed so many different methods of learning, and everything he learned made it easier for him to learn more because of what he already knew. Instead of a chicken-and-egg problem, Brody got into a *virtuous cycle of learning*. So today, eight years into his coaster obsession, he is able to read, watch, and understand incredibly complex concepts in physics and engineering when they are applied to roller coasters, because he has such a strong foundation of knowledge about them.

Not long ago I watched Brody transfer this approach to music. For three years he had been in the school band, learning to play trombone. Like many kids, upon reflection he was a little disappointed in his first pick of instrument, and wished he'd chosen clarinet. He got some pushback when he said he wanted to switch instruments, so instead of giving up trombone he decided to teach himself to play clarinet. He had a basic understanding of how you learn to play an instrument from his experience at school, and he'd also learned some fundamentals of music. Given all he'd discovered on his own about roller coasters, he felt confident he could access lessons to teach himself clarinet.

What's particularly interesting to me about Brody's story is that his exposure to roller coasters came when he was playing at a friend's house and got interested in a toy. His exploration of the clarinet was powered by the Internet. Brody's "sparks" required two things: time and access. The absence of either would have blocked his pursuit. And yet, we block time and access all the time without really thinking about it.

Increasingly competitive college admissions create one obstacle, in that kids feel pressured to become better at something than their peers. While there is nothing wrong with learning and becoming great at something—in fact, there is much right with it—there are trade-offs. Developmentally, young children don't really know themselves well enough or have a solid enough understanding of the world to know that one particular activity, like soccer, will be their enduring and primary interest for the next fourteen years. And for most, the commitment it takes to become good enough to stand out means that time after school, during evenings, and on weekends is largely consumed with that activity. Little room is left for other pursuits, especially those like free playing, that seem as if they aren't meaningfully productive. For instance, for years, Rett has been fascinated by maps. He can sit for hours creating detailed maps of imaginary lands. I have no idea where this interest is going—will he be a cartographer one day? A fantasy novelist?—It doesn't matter. The point is, he needs the time and space to explore it, and in doing so explore his interests and who he is. The object of his time invested in maps is not to define a career or even a major, the object is to learn how to learn by following his curiosity, and to figure out who he is and what he's interested in—the "ings"—along the way.

EXPOSE, EXPLORE, PURSUE

At Summit we put a lot of thought into *exposing* students to as many experiences and ideas as possible. Exposure provides the spark of interest. Part of that involves simply encouraging everyone, from teachers to students, to share their own interests and passions. The school hallways are filled with signs, posters, pictures, clothing, and stickers showing how members of the community are involved with a wide variety of topics, from knitting to politics. Individuals from outside of Summit are regularly invited to engage with the school, in ways ranging from presenting at future fairs to evaluating student projects. While these are small moments of exposure, we also have larger programs worked in to our curriculum, such as the camping trip we take as a school each year, and our annual Study Trips, wherein an entire class takes an immersive, interdisciplinary field trip that incorporates a college visit.

Most schools work hard to expose students to ideas, interests, and experiences. Exposure alone isn't enough, though, and so we offer students opportunities to *explore* what interests them—so a spark of interest about an abundance of dead dry trees on our camping trip, for instance, turns into a Passion Project wherein the student spends weeks or months studying forest fires and giving a TED-like talk on how they intend to make an impact. Our real-world, project-based approach to learning gives kids a ton of opportunities and choice within the projects to explore knowledge that's interesting to them.

Finally, students have opportunities to more deeply *pursue* what they really start to get excited about. This pursuit happens during Expeditions. You can think of Expeditions sort of like electives, except instead of taking five classes and an elective each semester, students at most Summit schools have eight weeks of immersive experiences that are blocked off in two-week chunks throughout the school year. During this time, they are able to choose from a wide array of electives we offer—for example, dramatic arts, film, photography, robotics, leadership training, and psychology, among many more courses in STEAM (the acronym encompassing science, technology, engineering, art, and mathematics), Well-Being, Future Planning, and Leadership & Society fields. They are also able to participate in an internship for valuable work experience, like David did when he worked at the tech company.

The Expeditions team publishes a descriptive "catalogue" of all the possibilities. It isn't a catalogue in the traditional sense, but rather a dynamic website that includes each option, a description of what you will do in the course, a short video about it, and examples of previous projects or student testimonials. We have a fair where all of the Expeditionary leaders are available to meet and discuss their area with prospective participants, and we've seen that often people become interested in something when they are drawn to a person who is interested or passionate about it. We let the students choose what interests them from a varied group of options.

Two other important and interesting twists to Expeditions are: 1) students can propose designing their own, and 2) some of the offerings are led by students. Even with a very lengthy list, we know we could never offer students opportunities to pursue everything they might be interested in. And so we encourage students to design their own experiences, either for themselves or for a group of peers. We ask them to meet the same standards we hold for our professional Expeditionary leaders. We give them support in planning and proposing their ideas, and when they meet the bar, we're thrilled.

The students enter the Expeditions experience with an interest and openness because they've chosen something meaningful to them. In some cases, after their first Expedition, kids will discover they're not all that interested after all, but others will be eager to continue on, often choosing to pursue the same subject for the whole year, or even on their own.

One student, Mishka, was captivated by film, and year after year, he designed film experiences for his Expeditions. When he graduated, he went to college to study film, and just recently came back to film Summit as a set for a documentary he's making. At a young age, he had the space, time, and encouragement to pursue his interest, which became his passion.

When Jimmy Zuniga was a junior at Summit, he partnered with two other students to propose an Expedition. Jimmy and his friends really wanted a Model UN group at Summit, but couldn't find a teacher who had the time to invest in leading it. The students had done a bunch of work to figure out what was required, and asked if they could design their own Expedition, but not just for themselves. They proposed designing a Model UN course they would teach to their peers, just like any other Expedition offering. I was ecstatic, as this was exactly the type of pursuit we wanted to promote. I could only imagine what a powerful perspective-changing experience it would be for the three student leaders, and what an incredible model it would be for their peers. Other members of our team tasked with ensuring legal and regulatory compliance were far less excited. It took a good deal of thought and work on our part to enable a student-led

Expeditionary experience that was both legal and safe, but we found a way.

We also were clear it would only work if we held Jimmy and his peers to the exact same standards we have for our other Expeditionary teachers and courses. They agreed and eagerly accepted the challenge. We provided them very clear expectations for course development and facilitation, and they had access to the same faculty member who coached teachers on lesson planning. I think back to what Jimmy learned about himself during that experience and the "ings" he figured out, and know the knowledge directly impacted the path he has chosen. Early in high school he shadowed our CFO and thought he wanted to be her one day. But experiences like his Model UN helped Jimmy realize he liked helping students, he liked lesson planning, giving feedback, and witnessing the lightbulbs going off when something finally clicked for someone. These were "ings" he didn't find in finance.

Not all kids are like Mishka and Jimmy. In fact, very few find something they know they love and follow it so early on. Most people have to be exposed to a really wide variety of subjects and often explore a multitude of dead ends before they find something they want to pursue. The benefit of this process? They're learning all along.

AUTHENTICITY MAKES THE DIFFERENCE

Exposing kids to potential areas of interest is tricky, even if they're not spending every free moment practicing their tennis serve or violin. Most kids need to consider many possibilities before finding one or more to explore. As a parent it can be really frustrating to see your child cycle through one potential interest after another. You might worry they don't have an ability to stick with something. Trying out new things can also be logistically and financially challenging. Oftentimes the only way to try something is to sign up for a class, camp, or series of lessons that must be paid for up front with little more than a short description of what the experience is about. When a child doesn't want to go back after the first time, the parent is put into the uncomfortable position of making the child do something she doesn't want to do, or letting her quit. Neither feels good. When at all possible, we want to expose kids to possible interests in ways that are efficient, but that will also pique their curiosity and motivate them to explore.

Consider something as simple as the selection of a book, for instance. It is very common for both teens and adults to pick up a book, look at the front and back cover for a minute, and then set it back down. But if someone is present who shares that he's read the book and why he liked it, a number of people will pick it back up again. They know more than they did before their friend intervened. If they're still not interested, they only spent a few minutes—not a big loss. And if they do in fact go on to read it but find it boring, again it's not a huge loss. The cost of cycling through ten books is pretty low in comparison to ten activities. But the notion holds that we want to find the right amount of exposure to identify a real motivation to explore. It might be a one-week summer camp focused on costume design, if the stars align.

But it also might be a crafts book, or even an hour watching an episode of *Project Runway Junior* to see if maybe, possibly, they want to watch another one.

The key is that we want our kids to explore an *authentic* curiosity and not a manufactured or mandated one, which is an easy trap to fall into. In a recent conversation with a friend, my friend asked for my thoughts on advice she had been given from a very expensive and popular college counselor. This counselor was well known for her ability to "get kids into top colleges" and she advised parents and high school freshmen to pick something and stick with it year after year, all the way through high school. This is rational advice, and comes directly from what college admissions officers say, which is they don't want kids with a long list of clubs and activities they know were fairly superficial. Rather, they want kids who go deep on something and show their persistence and passion for it, as well as their mastery.

The intention here was right. But unfortunately, the "hack the system" mindset led to a really distorted implementation. The counselor didn't really care if the kids felt authentically connected to the subject they chose—that wasn't the point. It just needed to be something that resonated with college admissions, and so she picked the activity for the kids based upon what she thought the colleges would want to see. "I'm a bit ashamed to tell you this," my friend said, "but I tried that approach, too. When I was in high school, and this was a while ago, I got advice from a counselor who said it would look really good to the college I wanted to attend if I started something on my campus. It would make me look entrepreneurial. So I created this program where I said I would match kids with volunteer opportunities. They could submit requests to me with their interests and I would match them up. Honestly, though, the whole thing was pretty half-assed because I was only doing it to get into college." The irony is my friend was the editor of her school newspaper and was totally passionate about that. She reveled in being in charge of a final product and orchestrating all the pieces it took to get there. "I loved every part of it and spent tons of time on it because I loved it," she said. Today she's a project manager who works in publishing. "Why didn't the counselor advise me to go deep into the thing I loved?" she wondered. "Instead I felt guilty about spending time on the paper and not my made-up interest." It's a good question, and the only answer I have is: when we confuse acceptance to a school or a job with preparedness for them, we miss the mark. When we prepare for not a specific school or job, but for the life we want, we tend to get *both* acceptance and fulfillment. We don't have to compromise.

THE POWER OF THE INTERNET

One of the most powerful tools in this quest to expose kids to possible passions is, of course, the Internet. I hesitate to even make that statement because there are legitimate downsides to devices and Internet access for our kids. While I acknowledge the real risks of being online, the unprecedented opportunity is unquestionable.

Summit students rely on technology as a tool to chart their growth, to conduct research for their projects, and more. Not surprisingly, we get a lot of questions from prospective parents about it. They worry about their child's time in front of a screen, and perceive that we're leaning on technology to do the heavy lifting. Our response to these questions reflects an approach to technology that is pragmatic (the Internet isn't going anywhere, so we need to teach kids to use it responsibly), and optimistic (there's much we can all gain when we leverage technology). It's an incarnation of the Google buffet: curate options, then give choice within it.

The Internet is a place where kids can seek information to inform their curiosity. In the same way a few minutes of book-talk can make a huge difference in hooking someone's interest in a way a book cover cannot, a short video can draw a child into something he wants to explore. Exploration online is easy with powerful search tools and one link leading to another. Of course, this is exactly what concerns parents who don't want their child to unwittingly link to a site that's inappropriate or even harmful.

But the Internet can also be a safe place for our children, with our engagement, guidance, and—at least at first—some parental controls in place. In the process of engaging with our kids online, we prepare them for when they will inevitably be on their own in the World Wide Web. Jordan Shapiro's book *The New Childhood: Raising Kids to Thrive in a Connected World* makes the argument that instead of taking a highly controlled approach with technology, parents engage in tech use with their kids. If Shapiro's kids are watching a horrible YouTube video that celebrates consumerism, he told NPR, "I want to have the conversation about why I find this attitude so weird and problematic, and I want to teach them to think about it that way. So now after having lots of these conversations, the first thing they do with every YouTube video they watch is ask, Who paid for it, what are they trying to sell me?"[4]

Equally important, from our experience of partnering with educators and communities across forty states, we are seeing firsthand the power of the Internet to eliminate geographic and socioeconomic barriers and limitations to exposure and exploration. For people living in smaller towns or rural areas, the Internet provides access to an entire world of potential interest, in the way libraries always have, that would never be possible in their physical location. But even in a city like New York, exposure is still limited by what you can get to and afford. Online, kids aren't limited to the common interests usually offered in schools and communities. Rather they can find information on anything, no matter how big or small, and the cost of cycling through possible interests is very low.

Recognizing the evolution and opportunity of technology, the American Academy of Pediatrics revised their recommendations for screen time in 2016, but this change is not well known. They no longer recommend specific limits to the amount of screen time kids six and older should have each day. Rather, they recommend each family create a media-use plan that designates media-free times (such as dinner) and locations (such as bedrooms), as well as defining reasonable limits to use so sleep, exercise, and social activity aren't replaced by screen time.[5] Parents can also play a huge role in modeling what it means to be curious, explore, and learn online.

KNOWLEDGE STILL MATTERS

Modeling curiosity also involves helping kids make connections between seemingly finite pieces of information and a bigger picture. For instance, when ten-year-old Ellie asked her parents, "Why do I have to know we have fifty states?" their best answer was "Just because." Most parents would probably have the same gut instinct about this fact and many more, but our kids clearly don't, and "just because" doesn't do much other than provoke the natural human instinct to press against something that doesn't make sense to you.

Ellie's question was actually a great opportunity for her parents to provide context. They could think of *why* knowing that fact was important to something they'd read or thought about lately. For example, a huge snowstorm was expected throughout five midwestern states, which would slowly travel all over the country. To understand the ramifications of the storm, Ellie's parents needed to understand what percentage of the country it would physically affect, so they could have couched her question in those terms. The Super Bowl was also on the horizon, and it would be hard to grasp the magnitude of the competition without a firm grasp of the league divisions that are grounded in the far reach of our country.

If we can't answer "why" questions because we don't know, then it's an invitation to codiscover and get curious *with* our kids, often by using our devices to access the Internet. What happens when we sit down with our child and genuinely seek an answer to a question neither of us knows the answer to? For starters, we get to demonstrate for them how to responsibly use our technology to advance our learning. We also demonstrate how to collaborate with one another. We create something authentic to talk about and the opening for conversations about what we value and how we make sense of the world. Most important, our kids get to see us as learners ourselves.

chapter Ten

Universal Skills:
The Innovation Summit

By Summit's ninth year, it had grown and developed tremendously. We had four Summit schools and two more preparing to open. All named after mountains, they were constant reminders of the climb both our students and our organization made in the quest to reach our ultimate goals. We had long waiting lists and stacks of letters from parents asking if we would open a Summit in their neighborhood. The rickety carriage we'd built in our first year had been transformed. Unlike the making of Cinderella's horse-drawn chariot, it hadn't happened instantly or through the flick of a magic wand. Nearly a decade of focused, hard work, and an orientation toward relentless improvement had turned Summit's schools into places that consistently and reliably transported every student on their learning journey.

Five classes of students had finished high school and those from our first class would graduate again, this time from college. Many were going to get their college diploma, but not all, and our entire organization came together to tackle the problem. Fifty-five percent of Summit's first graduates would earn a bachelor's degree that year. That was twice the national average and nearly eight times greater for our low-income and minority students. It surpassed all expectations Kimberly had had for our kids. Summit was being celebrated in national rankings, but we were uncomfortable. We *knew* the 45 percent of our students who hadn't yet completed a four-year degree. It didn't matter that most high schools did half as well, at best. To us, it was never about being relatively better, it was always about every student. To us, having all of our students succeeding truly meant *all*. Fifty-five percent wasn't good enough.

We interviewed our Summit alumni and knew that some of our students had chosen two-year degree programs and others had opted into career pathways like becoming journeyman electricians. Some had encountered the very real challenges of the high cost of college or low availability of courses in state schools and were taking much longer as a result. There were valid life reasons why not all of our kids had earned a four-year degree, and we could have used them as excuses. Instead, we chose to challenge ourselves. We heard time and again from our students who didn't stay in college that our high expectations for all students had indeed led them to college, but that we had "supported" them too much along the way. In moments when our students were stumbling, or at risk of failing, we would often metaphorically pick them up and carry them over the line. We may have gotten them to the next milestone, but in the process we deprived them of developing the skills they would need to do this for themselves. When they arrived at college and we were no longer there, many of them faltered.

The gut-wrenching part of this feedback was that it resonated so strongly as truth. We supported our students as much as we did because we loved them and would do anything in our power to help them succeed. Yet even while we were doing it, deep in our guts, we knew there were going to be issues later. Just as parents so often do, we rationalized our choices by saying if we didn't step in now, they didn't even have a chance at the future. And we were right, in many cases, to have done so; we couldn't let them fail big. But we could have let them fail small along the way, supporting them as they learned. We decided to go back to the drawing board and figure out what more we could do to prepare our students for the very real world they were encountering.

INNOVATION SUMMIT

A pop song provided upbeat background music to the growing buzz as nearly eighty educators entered Summit Prep, greeting each other with hugs and high fives while they grabbed coffee. A giant husky mural painted by our first class adorned the entryway and rows of college pennants hung from the tall rafters of the big open space. Our students were out, immersed in their Expeditions experiences, which allowed their teachers to spend this professional time together.

The next forty-eight hours were going to be intense. We had named the two-day design experience the Innovation Summit—pun intended. It was the kickoff to what would become an incredibly productive and profound month of professional work.

We didn't waste time getting started. Within a few minutes, everyone was randomly assigned to one of thirteen design teams, and we were off. The first order of business: stake out and quickly construct a "design studio" where a team of six could work for the next two days. Teachers and principals shuffled through a giant pile of gathered supplies that included everything from rolling whiteboards to shipping crates, beanbag chairs, blankets, and pillows. In a matter of minutes, all of the teams had formed and created funky and creative spaces to work. They were armed with a bucket of Post-its, markers, butcher paper, and random craft supplies.

Adam had traded in his bullhorn for a microphone. Now the chief academic officer for Summit, he had spent over a year building buy-in and support for this day. He worked closely with a coach, Frederick, who stood next to him. Frederick worked in the infamous "Garage" at Google and had extensive experience helping teams of people use a design process to find solutions to big problems. He had generously volunteered his time to help us.

Since Summit's beginning, for every decision we made, we'd asked ourselves, "What is best for kids?" Repeated so often, the question had become a mantra, a touchstone that kept us grounded in what was most important. On this day, we would take it a step further. Usually we asked what was best for kids within a specific context: What daily schedule was best? Which project? What teaching assignments and start time? This month, we had plans to zoom much further out and ask a bigger question: If we had absolutely no constraints, what school design would be best for kids?

Frederick had helped to conceive of a design-a-thon. It began with empathy; we sought to really understand everything about our students and the context of their lives. Every team had all of the data we could gather about our graduates and their experiences, as well as feedback and input from our current students.

The teams had a little time to prepare for the first interviews with students, who ranged in age from nine to eighteen. Over the two days they would interview the students, some from Summit, some not, several times. Frederick and Adam coached them to approach the interviews with a "child-like mind," filled with wonderment and interest at everything they heard. They cautioned against talking very much or asking long or loaded questions. Instead, they advised the teams to simply ask, "Why?" At first many of the kids seemed a bit unsure about sharing. But it didn't take long to get them talking. The teams quickly found out that kids have *a lot* to say about school and what works and doesn't work for them. I was captivated by the observations and ideas coming from a fifth grader named Kai who attended a local school. School wasn't working for him, a fact the team interviewing him couldn't comprehend at first. He came across as an incredibly insightful, communicative, polite, and funny young boy. How could it be that he felt he didn't belong at his school, hated going, and wondered if school was even for him? They managed to stick to the script and as they continued to ask why, they discovered Kai had a rich and wonderful family life and a well-developed fantasy world in his mind. He was curious and asked lots of questions his teacher didn't have time for or appreciate. The assignments she gave him felt frustrating and boring. He wasn't at all sure how he was benefiting from school.

Over the next two days, the teams toggled back and forth between interviewing kids and designing ideas based upon what they heard. Every time the kids returned, they would react to the team's proposals and prototypes, and when the kids left again, the teams worked to make them better. Kai's feedback nearly devastated the team the first time he returned. While they had gotten one key idea right—kids needed opportunities to explore interests—they had missed the boat entirely in Kai's mind. He wanted to know: How was their plan really helping him? Just letting him study something he was interested in didn't seem like a good reason to go to school.

Adam and Frederick kept morale up and helped when teams got stuck. At one point well into the first day, one team called a time-out to say what many were thinking: "The ideas we're coming up with are pretty different from what school looks like today. What if we do them and we're wrong? How can we responsibly experiment on our kids?" Where a moment before there had been a palpable energy, suddenly the big room went quiet.

Frederick, who was relatively soft-spoken and for the most part had been guiding from the side, stepped forward. He acknowledged the very real and serious tension of creating something different when people's lives were at stake.

And then he began to talk about his work on self-driving cars. "I think maybe it's not that different from school," he said. "We began work on self-driving cars to improve people's lives. Imagine if you could capture the time spent behind the wheel to do things you like to do. Imagine how much more relaxed you would be when you arrived at your destination. Self-driving cars could dramatically reduce traffic and eliminate the tens of thousands of accidents annually caused by driver error and distraction." He paused for a long moment, and then said, "And they're risky. At some point, our self-driving cars will have to begin practicing on the road. What if something goes wrong? What if they hurt someone? Or worse, what if they kill someone?" I felt myself holding my breath as I started to realize where Frederick was going with this. "Thirty thousand mothers, brothers, sisters, sons, daughters, and fathers die each year in America in preventable auto accidents. Have you ever lost anyone in a car accident? It seems unethical to do nothing if we can do something. But there is risk." He looked at us and asked, "Is it ethical for you to do nothing, when you know you can do something? How many sons and daughters will continue to be lost if you *don't* act?" The silence lingered long after he finished speaking. Slowly, people began to turn back to their groups. In hushed voices they began to wonder, *If we weren't preparing every child, which ones were we willing to lose?*

The teams went back to building their prototypes from pipe cleaners, clay, colored paper, and much more. Held together with tape and glue, the models were rough, but successfully conveyed big ideas for what school could look like if designed to truly serve our kids.

At the end of the second day, each team presented their new school model to an audience of students, parents, teachers, and community members. Then the competition began. Everyone received play money to invest in the school models they liked best, with students allotted more than adults. All those we'd interviewed returned with their parents. They could put every dollar on one or divide up their money as they saw fit. In the end, Team Nautilus, who had worked with Kai, won. Kai's specific and honest feedback had been hard to hear, but the team didn't shy away. They'd thrown out their first prototype, let go of their old ideas, and started building something Kai would love and respect. In the end, their design was called My Path and featured integrated learning experiences drawn from students' interests and passions, and clearly linked the experiences to the skills colleges and employers sought. Powered by an app, My Path allowed students to decide what they wanted to do in the future and then showed how everything they learned and did in school would get them ready. After careful consideration and a long hard look at all of the options, Kai had put all his money on My Path.

On one level, it seemed obvious: School should prepare kids for the future they want. On another it seemed impossible. What if they all wanted different things? Wouldn't that be chaos? How could every student learn what they needed to learn if they all had different aspirations? The answer was a focus on universal skills.

A COORDINATED APPROACH

A month later, I stood with all of our teachers at Summit Everest high school, staring at the biggest wall we had in any of our buildings. We'd been working day in and day out since the Innovation Summit. The insights and inspiration we'd gained from our students and creative collaboration had fueled an effort to create a comprehensive *backward map* of the universal skills our students would need to be ready for college, career, and life. The wall was covered with our plan that had been printed on colored paper and littered with sticky notes. To most it probably looked like an aisle of Office Depot exploded. Kai and the other kids had helped us realize they wanted to know where they were going and how they were going to get there. To a teacher, a backward map is a teaching and learning plan that begins with the end clearly defined. What does the teacher expect her students will know and do at the conclusion of a learning experience, and what will they do along the way to get there? Backward mapping stands in stark contrast to teaching, which is simply a set of activities strewn together—the equivalent of driving around in your car without a destination. You might see something cool along the way, but the method is totally unreliable as a means to get you where you need to go.

From the beginning, Summit's teachers had backward-mapped the curriculum. Each teacher had worked diligently to develop projects and learning experiences that were a path to the end-of-year outcomes they expected from their kids. They had collaborated with their peers and sometimes even taught together, and so there was a lot of synergy among their plans, but there wasn't intentional alignment. In the end, each plan belonged to an individual teacher, who taught an individual course. Each course drove to different skills, and while potentially all were important, they weren't coordinated among subject areas, or consistent. So while sophomore history teacher Mr. Hall had a great project going with colonialism and introduced students to research skills, he'd never really talked to the junior history teacher about what research skills the kids needed in that class and how ready they had to be.

The isolation of teachers likely grew out of a history of teachers working alone in one-room schoolhouses. Then came the industrial model of schooling, which held that subject area teachers should teach just that subject area. But the solitary nature of the profession has likely persisted because of logistics—or rather, the plain truth that teachers simply do not have time to work with their colleagues. The vast majority of teachers have less than an hour a day when they are not working directly with students. Rarely will this hour be coordinated with the hour their colleagues have free. Beyond daily time, teachers often have as few as five or six days per year when they're not engaged with students and can gather to work with their peers. The real demands of teaching crowd the time they have and all but eliminate the chance to collaborate.

All of this means that most teachers decide what and how to teach without coordinating with the students' other teachers. From the students' perspective, this means they encounter five to six different perspectives a day about what they should learn. When compounded over the four years of high school, a student will have been subjected to at least twenty different interpretations of the skills, knowledge, and habits they should be developing. And as the evaluators of students and thus the gatekeepers for students' future options, teachers hold significant power in conveying what is important. Students behave rationally, focusing on what each teacher expects of them as opposed to developing universal skills to prepare for the future. How can students develop universal skills if there isn't a common agreement or approach to developing them?

The Innovation Summit had allowed us to go back and walk in the shoes of our students. In doing so, we were reminded that while each of our courses was well designed and driving toward important learning, they weren't all aligned and coherent for the student. This robbed kids of the opportunity to practice the most important skills year in and year out until reaching mastery. Naming skills different things and measuring them in different ways may not have seemed like a big deal to teachers. In the best cases they understood that developing a thesis to one teacher meant the same thing as making a claim to another. And when given time, they could look at one another's grading schemas and figure out how they were basically looking for something similar, even if they were using different words to explain it to students, and scoring what they saw differently. But recognizing the similarities ended with the teachers. Kids had no way of stringing these things together and so to them the courses and subjects were separate and disconnected. There wasn't a logical pattern or a clear message about what skills they would ultimately need to master.

What would it be like if we looked to athletics for inspiration? The world knows what a 100-meter dash is and there is agreement on how to measure a person's ability to run it. The world has a common understanding of how fast the fastest person is, and the speeds that are normal for a novice, and those that are normal for a professional. This means a ten-year-old in his local park, with the help of his parents, a timer, and a tape measure, can figure out exactly how fast he is. He can name his current athletic ability. More important, with that information, he can begin to do something about it. There are countless resources he can access to help him improve, and numerous choices he can make each day to determine if he gets better at the 100-meter dash. And while an expert running coach will likely accelerate the boy's improvement more than if the boy were to work on his own, with friends, or with parents, he is not solely dependent upon the expert to grow. We wanted to give our kids the same tools and the ability to work with our expert coaches on those all-important skills year after year. That required consensus, specificity, complete alignment about what the all-important *universal skills* were.

EMPLOYERS WANT UNIVERSAL SKILLS

For an athlete to do well in a sport, she'll need a generally accepted set of skills. While some are specific to a sport, like soccer, or a position, like pitcher, many cut across all sports.

Athletes in virtually every arena benefit from being cardio-vascularly fit, strong, and agile. The same is true for life, as just about everyone agrees skills like communication, critical thinking, and problem solving are pretty important. These broad skills make us feel someone's got what it takes, and make us want to hire them. Countless lists of what employers seek reflect these skills:

ATTRIBUTES EMPLOYERS SEEK ON NEW COLLEGE GRADUATES' RESUMES

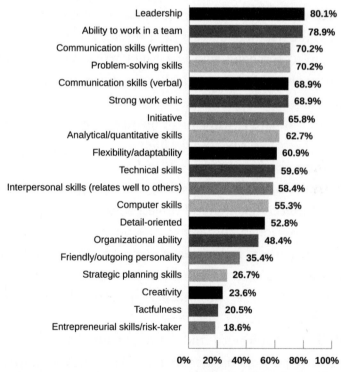

Attribute	Percentage
Leadership	80.1%
Ability to work in a team	78.9%
Communication skills (written)	70.2%
Problem-solving skills	70.2%
Communication skills (verbal)	68.9%
Strong work ethic	68.9%
Initiative	65.8%
Analytical/quantitative skills	62.7%
Flexibility/adaptability	60.9%
Technical skills	59.6%
Interpersonal skills (relates well to others)	58.4%
Computer skills	55.3%
Detail-oriented	52.8%
Organizational ability	48.4%
Friendly/outgoing personality	35.4%
Strategic planning skills	26.7%
Creativity	23.6%
Tactfulness	20.5%
Entrepreneurial skills/risk-taker	18.6%

0%   20%   40%   60%   80%   100%

Percentage of employers seeking listed skill

Source: National Association of Colleges and Employers.

This is a great list, and it's hard to argue with the importance of any of the attributes, but it's also pretty general. What *is* flexibility, exactly, and how do you know if someone has it? What does it mean to be a leader? How does that differ from being entrepreneurial? Is someone with initiative also a risk-taker? If Summit was to teach the universal skills, we had to be able to name, define, and measure them.

As we dug into the science and consulted with experts, we zeroed in on seven universal skill domains that met our criteria. Not only were they named, defined, and measurable, but they were also teachable. They weren't the big attributes reflected on the employer list, but when combined with one another, the habits of success, and specific knowledge, they added up to someone who is a leader, communicator, and problem-solver. I began to visualize the universal skills, habits of success, and knowledge as Legos that could be assembled in all different ways to ultimately give a person the high-level attributes needed for life.

So, from the premise that all teachers would focus on developing the same universal skills, we mapped out over two hundred projects spanning all subject areas. Each project was carefully positioned throughout a student's experience to build on the others and enable students to practice the same skill over and over to drive real improvement, in the same way a baseball player will practice his swing day after day, and year after year.

We knew that when a student started ninth grade at Summit, she would work on the universal skill of using sources a dozen times—enough to give her meaningful practice. She'd work on it all four years in English and history, and in her

ThE UnIVErSaL SKILLS RUbrIC

Projects across subject area courses
are assessed on these 36 skills:

Textual Analysis	Theme/Central Idea Point of View/Purpose	Development Word Choice	Structure
Products & Presentations	Communicating Accurately and Precisely	Multimedia in Communication	Oral Presentation
Inquiry	Asking Questions Defining a Design Problem	Planning and Carrying Out Investigations	Hypothesizing
Analysis & Synthesis	Organizing and Representing Information Identifying Patterns and Relationships Comparing/Contrasting Modeling	Interpreting Data/ Info to Make Valid Claims Making Connections & Inferences Evaluating Arguments	Evaluating Competing Design Solutions Constructing a Design Solution Constructing an Evidence-based Explanation
Speaking/ Listening	Contributing to Evidence-based Discussions	Norms/Active Listening	
Composing/ Writing	Argumentative Claim Informational/ Explanatory Thesis Narrative Counterclaims	Selection of Evidence Explanation of Evidence Integration of Evidence	Organizations (Transitions, Cohesion, Structure) Introduction and Conclusion
Using Sources	Selecting Relevant Sources	Contextualizing Sources	Synthesizing Multiple Sources

second and third year in science. We could follow the trajectory all the way through.

Putting the giant wall together wasn't easy. For good reason, teachers love their autonomy and ability to decide what they teach. While every teacher wanted what was best for our students and agreed a coordinated approach that looked not at a single teacher or subject but at the curriculum as a whole was the right course, they had to give up a lot to get it. That month had included fierce debates about exactly which skills were universal, how to best describe them, and the most effective ways to develop students. Teachers had given impassioned speeches about why certain subjects were different from one another and deserved different universal skills, only to be questioned by peers on the meaning of a universal skill. We spent a good deal of time debunking some tightly held beliefs about learning that are unsupported by science and evidence.

In the end, our teachers are professionals, and the mantra "What's best for kids?" was as natural to them as breathing. The plan on that giant wall answered the question by saying, "What's best for kids is we make transparent the universal skills they need to become successful adults. What's best for kids is for us to spend every minute of every day helping them to develop and grow those skills."

What happened over the course of that month was basic and yet revelatory, academic and yet seismic. We would never have gotten there, never have been able to approach skills with such an open mindset, had we not had the experience of Innovation Summit—which asked us to consider what we would do if we weren't afraid.

A CELEBRATION OF LEARNING

It was Celebration of Learning night at Summit. Each student had a designated spot where they could share their most recent work. Depending upon the projects they'd been working on, their final products varied. They had essays, models, and multimedia presentations. Some had their notes from Socratic seminars they'd been in and others played recordings of the speeches they'd given. They shared pictures from mock trials, letters to political figures, and artwork created using math equations. It was impressive to see the caliber and quality of work by all of the kids, but the highlight for me was their reflections. Each student was ready to discuss the goals they'd set for the project (Which specific skills were they working on? Why?), the plan they'd made, how it had gone, the growth they had experienced, where they still needed to work, and what learning they were taking as they moved to their next project.

"When I started the Crash Course project," Jackie, a dark-haired, freckled sophomore, said as she shared the episode she had written and filmed, "I was strong at the skill of making an argumentative claim. But I really needed to work on my organization. Specifically, my transitions. I also wanted to improve my skill of selecting relevant sources. I had struggled with that in my last project." The people surrounding her—including a few parents and some younger siblings—nodded and glanced at one another, signaling how impressed they were.

No matter how many times I had these conversations, it always took me a minute to realize I was talking to a high school kid. Argumentative claim, transitions, selecting relevant sources . . . who talks like that? How did Jackie even know what she was good at? But, of course, she knew because she'd practiced, and she'd been taught the language that would help her track her skill progression. She had practiced the same skills day in and day out, not in just one class, but in every class, and not just for one year, but every year.

"You said you set a goal to improve selection of relevant sources," I asked her. "What did you do to improve that skill?" I love asking kids this question, because they go off script, and it's clear they're now just talking about what they do every day, and not performing for the parents who've come to see their work. They'll talk about the mistakes they made, the feedback they got, how they worked with their teachers and peers and at some point something clicked and they started to make some progress. This was what Jackie explained, in great detail. In her case, she hadn't really realized that media sources can be biased and have different standards. She began to learn how to do a bit of research on the sources of her information, not to rule them out necessarily, but to understand everything from their funding to their mission. Understanding who was behind the information she was counting on to be factual and accurate was important as she weighed differing opinions and conflicting accounts.

Others might answer my question by explaining they didn't get as far as they wanted to get and they need to keep working. They're optimistic. They know another project is coming where they'll get another chance to practice the skill they need to work on. And all of them have something they do well. There are no A, B, or C students on these nights. Every conversation is unique, and at the same time they all have something in common. Everyone has something they do well. And everyone has something they're working on. When people are solving real problems, answering big questions, and doing real work, it's never perfect. That's not the point. It's always about growth.

Chapter Eleven

Concrete Next Steps:
Life After Graduation

One warm spring afternoon in 2007, I felt lighter than I had in years. Most days of my past four years had been filled with stress, worry, and lots of hard problems as I'd worked to build Summit Prep. But on this day I felt an ease; we were celebrating. The group of students I'd mentored for four years was graduating. This was our final meeting, and so we'd made a party out of it and walked to the local IHOP for lunch. We'd become like a family over the previous four years. Our closeness was on full display as we ambled back toward campus, laughing, joking, and teasing one another.

I don't know who first noticed the man waiting at the locked door to the Summit office. The man was Latino, in his late twenties, and there was something familiar about him, but I had no idea who he was.

As we approached he looked at me for a long time and then slowly raised his hand in recognition and relief. I walked up the ramp to the door where he stood, my mentees lined up like ducklings behind me. They were a curious group and always in one another's business, including mine.

As I reached the man, he said, "Ms. Shafer? I mean, Ms. Tavenner?"

And suddenly it clicked. He had been one of my students at Hawthorne. "Mateo?" I asked hesitantly.

"Yes," he said, relieved. He brought his hand to his heart in a gesture I remembered well. "I had to find you."

"Is everything okay?" Sadly, I'd been conditioned to assume the news about my students from Hawthorne would be bad.

"Yes. Everything is great," he spoke quickly. "I'm here in the Bay Area with my family and I had to come and find you to thank you."

"Oh," I said, surprised. "For what?"

I'd first met Mateo when he was a sophomore at Hawthorne, assigned to my college prep English class. He was a solid student who always completed his assignments and respectfully participated in class. On occasion he would hang back and we would talk about the novels we were reading or about life in general, and I discovered he had a sense of humor, a girlfriend, and dreams of being the first in his family to go to college. I was the faculty adviser for the student newspaper and recruited Mateo to join. Over the next two years he became one of my most reliable and diligent reporters. In the fall of his senior year, he asked me to help him apply to a state university and I was surprised to see he didn't have the grades to be admitted. He'd been a very strong student in my class, but his transcript showed his performance across other classes was uneven. He was disappointed by the realization, but bounced back. In June of 1998, when he graduated from Hawthorne High School, his plan was to attend the local community college for two years and then transfer to a state university.

The morning after Mateo's graduation, I had returned to school to pack up my classroom for the last time, as I was about to join Scott in Northern California. The campus was a disaster from the party the night before—banners celebrating the Class of 1998 were strewn about, and the confetti and streamers had grown damp in the morning mist, creating a soggy, sad-looking mess. I averted my eyes from the mess and got to work when I heard a knock. Mateo stood in the doorway. "Hey, Ms. Shafer—I mean, Ms. Tavenner." The kids were still having a hard time getting used to my married name.

"Hey, Mateo, what's up?" I was happy to see him, but a little bit worried. What was he doing here the morning after graduation?

"I thought I'd come by to see if you needed any help?" Something was definitely wrong. I could tell by his tone and how he didn't look me in the eye.

"Thanks. That's generous of you. Yeah, I could use some help with these boxes," I said, trying to play it cool. He'd tell me what was going on if I gave him room.

Head hung, Mateo walked toward me and suddenly stopped. "I came to tell you, I'm not going to college."

"Oh, why?" I asked with a mixture of surprise and confusion.

"I just think I need to work. You know, my mom has been supporting me all these years and she needs my help." He glanced up and I caught his eye.

"Why did you decide to come and tell me, Mateo?" I asked. He held my gaze, but didn't answer. Finally, I broke the silence and said, "I think you came here because you know I'm not going to let you make that decision. Come on. Let's go." Mateo followed me to my car and we drove to the local community college. We walked the campus, went to the registration office, filled out all of the paperwork, selected classes, and enrolled him on the spot. We went to the bookstore and bought Mateo's books and finally we found the classroom where his first class would be held. The door was unlocked. We walked inside, sat in the front row of desks, and imagined what it would be like for Mateo to be a student there.

We spent just four hours together that day, and I didn't remember it until Mateo stood waiting outside my locked door ten years later. The truth is, I hadn't considered our interaction around his future to be special. It was just part of being a teacher. It was what all of us did.

"I had to come and tell you I'm a teacher now," Mateo said. "I finished community college and transferred, just like we planned, and I earned my degree. I knew I needed to help other kids like me. Now I'm teaching at Hawthorne in the same classroom you taught me in." A loud "whoa" escaped from my mentees, who'd been intently watching our reunion. "I'm trying to do for other kids what you did for me," he finished abruptly.

I hadn't realized it, but at some point during his explanation I'd begun to cry. The students I had been mentoring closed in behind me and I felt their encouragement. I was at a loss for words, and so I hugged him. When I'd been Mateo's teacher, I certainly didn't hug students. At first he was a bit surprised, and then he relaxed into the embrace and we laughed.

I couldn't stop thinking about that moment for weeks. How many people had helped me in my life whom I had never thanked? I'd had several turning point moments, and people and opportunities had crossed my path that enabled me to take a road out of Lake Tahoe and drive myself to college. When I'd been Mateo's age, my high school teacher had knocked on my door one late-summer day. I was supposed to leave for college in four days—a college that I'd never seen except in photos, and that was five hundred miles away. She said, "Diane, pack your things. You need to leave tonight."

I tried to argue with her, but she gently took me by the shoulders and said, "You are leaving tonight. You are getting in that car you worked so hard to buy. You are taking the $254 you have managed to save and you are driving out of this town." She had lost two students that year—one to suicide, one to a drunk driving accident. So on some level I understood when she said, "You are packing your bags and going right now, because I'm not going to lose another one of you to this town." I had done what she said.

I had other people who had come into my life, too, but I'd never sent a note, never called, and certainly never driven five hundred miles and tracked them down ten years later to let them know they'd changed the trajectory of my life. Why didn't I do that? The joy of seeing Mateo was nearly drowned out by my feelings of regret and guilt. I didn't deserve Mateo's thanks. I didn't do anything special. I just did my job, like so many other teachers I knew.

In the few moments I shared with Mateo, I realized so many important things. The little everyday actions by teachers matter. Our beliefs about what our kids are capable of, and our willingness to be uncompromising in helping them see what is possible, matter. It is the personal connection and seeing someone for who they are and what they want that enables them to become who they are and to know themselves. Clearly the little things had made a huge difference to Mateo. Someone had been there for me, I'd been there for Mateo, and now he was going to be there for countless other kids. As beautiful as the paying it forward was, though, it wasn't enough. What about the kids who didn't have someone to push them through their moments of doubting their plans? What about the kids who didn't have a plan at all?

SUMMER MELT

Today, there is a term for what almost happened to Mateo. It's called "the summer melt." It's used to describe a national phenomenon of what happens to as many as 40 percent of kids who graduate high school each year intending to start a four-year or community college in the fall, but who don't.[1] Rather, these hundreds of thousands of students melt away in the summer.[2] It could be that they missed an important enrollment deadline, became overwhelmed with the paperwork involved with their financial aid, or just felt they needed to help support their family. If you consider that fewer than 70 percent of kids who graduate from high school plan to attend college in the first place, and that of the ones who do go, 30 percent of those don't make it to their sophomore year, we have a system that is dropping kids fast, so that the climb to a college degree is via a slope of slippery ice.

Over the years at Summit, 7 percent of our graduates have melted in the summer after graduation. One student is one too many, and so we are committed to understanding the underlying causes and finding a solution. Using a disciplined approach for constantly improving our schools, we have deeply engaged our students, our graduates, and the scientists who best understand this trend and its causes.

All of our work has led us to believe that in addition to habits of success, curiosity-driven knowledge, and universal skills, there is something else our students need to be truly prepared to live a fulfilled life. They need a *concrete next step*.

WHAT'S NEXT? BUILDING A NEXT STEP

Everyone in our nation can say they plan to go to college. The community college system in America allows virtually anyone to attend their local institution without meeting any entrance requirements. However, there is a big difference between saying you plan to go to college and actually engaging in the process to go to college. The differences show up in the extraordinarily low graduation rates—roughly 25 percent—for these institutions.[3]

Over the last decade or two, college planning has become

a key activity in high schools and within families across America. With data showing college graduates on average earn a million dollars more than high school graduates over their lifetime,[4] Americans have gotten the message: college is a ticket to financial stability. An entire industry is now dedicated to college acceptance. For the right price, families can get expert help for kids on college admissions exams, essay writing, application completion, and scholarship searches. Organizations and technology tools support college touring and college list making. Summer and afterschool programs are designed for kids to have experiences that will look good on their applications, and an abundance of guidebooks will tell them how to do it. We also have an industry focused on national rankings. Lists and lists of the best colleges are published annually with every twist imaginable—best colleges in the Northeast, best liberal arts colleges, best technical colleges, best research universities, and on it goes.

For their part, high schools employ college counselors, make classroom presentations, keep libraries of college catalogues, and sometimes pay for software students can use to help search for college options. More and more schools require ninth and tenth graders to take earlier versions of the admissions exams like the PSAT and ACT, and devote whole school days to college preparation. High schools host parent nights to talk about college and share information about the process and financial aid. They also hang college pennants throughout their campuses.

One of the results of all of this effort is that 90 percent of ninth graders today say they plan to go to college.[5] When asked why, they will most often say, "Because I want to be a doctor/lawyer/veterinarian." When pressed further as to why they want to be a vet, they might say, "Because I like animals," or something fairly vague. Next, adults usually ask, "Where do you want to go?" and students will respond with a geographic description—"I want to be in New York/ Boston/Kansas City" or something like "I want to stick close to home."

For the truly persistent questioner who asks which school they want to go to and why, if a student has an answer it generally falls into one of four buckets: 1) "A family member went there"; 2) "I'm a fan of the college's sports teams"; 3) "It's a really good school—it's generally ranked on one of the top-school lists"; or 4) "It has a beautiful campus." It's not surprising that all four responses are rooted in familiarity. The college is in some way known to the student. It's unlikely you'd want to go somewhere you don't know anything about, and while that's not surprising, it *is* limiting, especially for an investment that's so large. On average the cost of a four-year college degree today is $40,000[6] and 70 percent of students take on debt to earn the degree.[7] They also spend the first four to six years of adulthood at the college, living in this chosen community and within its values. And yet, I often find kids do more research and know more specific and detailed information about their first car than they do their college—the place they will first practice being an adult.

Perhaps this limited thinking about four-year colleges is due to the fact that it doesn't feel like much of a choice for many kids these days. Each year the statistics seem to tell an ever more daunting story to American students about how hard colleges are to get into. The percentage of straight-A, superstar athletes and leaders who get accepted to our nation's best colleges falls lower and lower each year, sinking into single digits for most of the top-ranked institutions. If these perfect kids can't get in, how is a mere mortal supposed to compete? The effects have been chilling. Today, most students and their families frame the college process by asking, "What school will accept me?" when the real question should be "What school will I accept?"

At Summit, we aim for every graduate to be accepted to, and enrolled in, a *best-fit experience that will propel them toward a fulfilled life.* For most of our students this will be college, for others it will be the military or a journeyman craftsman program or something else. We have important criteria for what it means to be a "best fit," as what our graduates choose to do next should be:

- Consistent with a vision they have created for their life as an adult based upon the knowledge they have of themselves
- Purposeful and realistic
- A fully informed choice from a set of real options
- Supported by family and community

Developing a concrete next step requires emerging adults to have a deep and specific sense of who they are and what they value. They also need knowledge of what the world has to offer. Most important, they need to understand the intersection between the two, so they can uncover best-fit options that make a good match.

The process to select a concrete step is not linear. Rather, students move back and forth and between six types of activities:

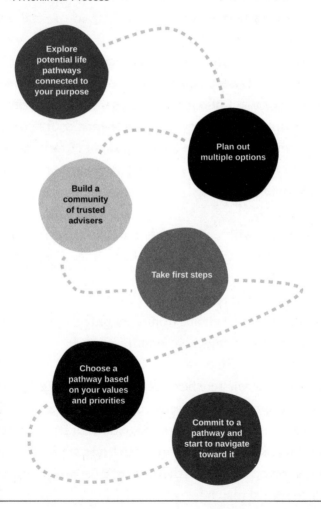

BUILDING CONCRETE NEXT STEPS
A Nonlinear Process

Explore potential life pathways connected to your purpose

Plan out multiple options

Build a community of trusted advisers

Take first steps

Choose a pathway based on your values and priorities

Commit to a pathway and start to navigate toward it

People begin by trying on different potential pathways—the *prototype purpose* phase. This can happen in the form of experiences, like job or school shadowing days, and also through meaningful dialogue with people who have already pursued an area of interest. In both cases, the prototyping happens as students reflect on their experiences, and can see and begin to imagine themselves on this pathway. Just as Mateo imagined himself in the college classroom, students need to mentally build a picture of themselves doing different things. The more colorful and complete the picture, the more they will be able to explore how it makes them feel and if it aligns with who they are and what they value. These insights are crucial as students begin to create options and ultimately make choices among them.

A good friend of mine likes to say, "Sometimes when you go wedding dress shopping, the first one you try on is the one." And while this certainly might be true, she is quick to point out that you won't know that until you've tried on dress two, three, four, and five. It's common for students to like the first experience they prototype and then to quickly cling to it. Bombarded with questions and pressure to know what they "want to be when they grow up," it is no wonder kids seek an answer they can give. The downside is that an initial commitment can prevent them from continuing to search and explore, and thus ultimately limit the options and choices they'll have. It's critical that kids *plan out multiple options,* even when they're resistant. At Summit, we require seniors to map out at least three plans, complete with degree, certificate, or experience opportunities they will pursue and how their skills and interests align with the opportunity.

They detail the process for taking the next step, the timeline, the cost, and why it is a good fit for them.

Rett and I recently had a conversation about this when he complained that he was required to create an alternate pathway plan at school. "I don't know why I can't try my first choice path and then make a new plan if it doesn't work," he said. We spent some time talking through the timing of the plans and how waiting might compromise opportunities. More important, the value of exploring a second plan became evident to us both when he shared what he had plotted: taking a gap year to work abroad given his interests in traveling and exploring. "I've just learned something about you," I told him. "I hadn't heard you explain that before. It's interesting thinking. Now that I know it, I can support you in exploring it."

One of the key aspects of prototyping multiple plans is that it allows students to talk about their ideas among their family, friends, and networks of support, through which they *build a community of trusted advisers*. They receive valuable feedback, opportunities to reflect, and inevitably, opportunities to gain support. A student might have nursing as one of her pathways, though it's not her primary choice. Her friend, on hearing this, says, "Oh, my aunt's a nurse. Why don't you give her a call?" In my experience there are countless people willing and able to support emerging adults. The biggest challenge is figuring out how. When plans begin to come out of kids' heads and into conversations, they start to make connections with people who can lead them to networks of support.

Each year at Summit we have at least a handful of seniors

who confidently know which path they want to take and exactly what they want to do. These students inevitably do not want to waste time or money applying for multiple options, and often are very resistant. Some of these kids are particularly hard-charging, so driven to get into their top choice of college that nothing else is acceptable. These kids need the multiple path assignment as much as—if not more than— anyone. Knowing that there is a plan B, or plan C, that is not only viable but that aligns with who they are and what they want to contribute in the world, lowers anxiety. It returns them to an understanding of their sense of self and sense of purpose that is so much richer than an SAT score or acceptance (or rejection) letter from their top-choice school.

There is value to *taking first steps* on the other extreme, too. For some students, rejection poses such a threat that they don't dare to apply for anything considered a reach. This was certainly true for Miguel when he was a member of Summit's first graduating class in 2007. He knew he wanted to become an electrician from the time he met the recruiter from the International Brotherhood of Electrical Workers (IBEW) at Summit's career fair. He didn't see any value in applying to college in his senior year, instead insisting he only needed to submit one application to the IBEW. This was long before we had formalized the concrete next steps requirement, and so Miguel's history teacher, Kelly Garcia, became very involved. She spent months in conversation with Miguel, finally resorting to asking him to apply to CSU East Bay as a favor to her. As they sat side by side completing the application, Miguel confided what a waste of time it was since he was never going to be accepted to college.

A few months later, when Miguel received his acceptance letter, he wondered out loud how it had happened. He was true to his ambition, though—he declined the university offer and pursued being an electrician instead. Ten years later, he admitted to me how annoyed he'd been with Kelly. "At the time I was so frustrated with you guys for making me apply to college. I knew I wasn't going to get accepted and it was going to be embarrassing, and then I did and I was so surprised. At the time, I couldn't even imagine going to college, but as I've gotten older and now have my own kids I think about it. I think I might like it. I'd like to learn electrical engineering and I think I might be able to do it now." Miguel paused for a moment and then said, "Well, I got accepted once, which means I probably could again. And even if I don't go to college, I know I want my kids to go. I know what they need to do and every day I'm talking to them about it."

There is so much wrapped up in Miguel's insights. His fears about not being wanted or accepted are ubiquitous among high schoolers today. How many of their choices and behaviors are driven by fear, by the fact they think no one will want them? Imagine the debilitating impact of that fear on their motivation. A disciplined process of creating a life plan that includes a concrete next step is the antidote. Engaging in real experiences, real data, and real self-exploration enables kids to flip the framing of their next stage of life so they feel empowered and in control, able to *navigate* themselves, as opposed to subject to the whims of big, impersonal institutions.

I'm glad Miguel applied to college, but he *chose well* when he decided to decline the offer. During his time at Summit, he worked closely with several mentors and really explored his "ings." He liked working with his hands. He did not like sitting at a desk. He liked feeling accomplished when he finished a task that made something better for someone or fixed something. He liked seeing the result of his work in practical use. He valued hard work. In geometry, math made sense for the first time because he could picture real objects. He liked stable, predictable work and a steady routine that left time for family and friends. He wanted to live in the Bay Area, where all of his family lives, and he wanted to buy a house. He wanted a career that would give him the financial chance to do so. He had tried several other construction-oriented jobs, like laying tile and landscaping. He worried about the toll they would take physically over many years and didn't like the lack of professional standards for those crafts. Miguel's mother was poor, and so Miguel was poor. He didn't want to be poor anymore, and couldn't imagine going into debt before he even started to work, which would have been necessary in order for him to go to college. Miguel knew himself and his values. He had explored what the world offered and he made an informed choice.

FROM BULGARIA TO THE NEXT STEP . . . AND THE NEXT

Bulgaria is not a place I would have chosen to travel, but I was invited to attend an international education conference focused on personalizing learning. The conference organizers really wanted students to be at the center of the conference experience, and so about a month before I was to fly there they called and asked if I could bring a Summit senior with me who would be willing to do a ten-minute talk on the ideas in the book *The End of Average* by Todd Rose. I gulped. I loved the idea of making students a big part of adult learning, but the logistics of travel to a small village in Bulgaria were such that I didn't feel comfortable taking a student on my own. I shared my hesitation and then posited, "Well, I guess I could bring my own son. He *is* a Summit student, but he's a ninth grader." They jumped at the offer. I was overcome with a sense of panic. What they wanted was a heavy lift for an adult. Creating a ten-minute talk and delivering it to an international audience was a big deal. I gathered my wits and said I couldn't speak for Rett, but I would ask him.

I sat on the corner of his bed and relayed the story. As I did, I watched a tiny smile creep to the corner of his mouth. I knew that look. It was a look that so clearly said, "I've been waiting for this moment." I found myself telling him how much work and how difficult this would be and that I wouldn't be able to help because I was traveling a lot. My words were designed to dissuade him because I was nervous. What if he said yes and then couldn't do it? What if we showed up and he failed? When I was honest about it, the worry came more from me looking bad if he failed than him having a bad experience. I didn't admit that, but it was true.

When I finally stopped, Rett said, "Yes."

"Yes, but did you hear what you have to do?" I asked incredulously.

"Mom, don't worry, I got this. This is what we do every

day at Summit. This is why you made Summit." I slumped back. He was right, and I was so very wrong.

The opportunity was in many ways a perfect fit for Rett. While not a lot of kids would voluntarily take on essentially another big school project, this one squarely aligned with Rett's sense of purpose. Growing up side by side with Summit has made him really interested in and passionate about education. He has a specific passion for international education that goes beyond mine. It comes from his deep curiosity about history, geography, and current events. During his three previous years he developed not only self-directed skills, as I was about to learn, but an emerging sense of his purpose in the world. When he was little, I would sometimes drag him with me to college classes where I was a guest lecturer or to recruiting events. He loved to listen, but what he really loved was talking and sharing his experience and views. The trip to Bulgaria offered an opportunity to combine so many of his specific and individual interests and as a result he threw himself into it.

He started by asking for help. Since I was to be gone, he sat down with his dad and asked if he could help him make a schedule so he would finish on time. Next he went to his mentor and together they identified the resources he could leverage at school. Pulling on all he had learned from doing projects and self-directing for three years, he knew how he learned best, so by the weekend he had both the audio and written version of *The End of Average* and worked his way through the book. It was the first time I was seeing him use the academic skills and habits of success he had been building at school in a nonschool context. He was leveraging his dad at home for support and his community at school for help as well. A few days before we were to depart he shared his speech with me via Google Docs. I was nervous as I opened it. My eyes widened as I read, and a sense of relief rushed over me. It was good. It was really good. But what was even more powerful was how many comments were in the document. His history and English teacher had both commented in the document and he had obviously asked them to help edit. He also had comments from several classmates. He was using his resources and they were responding with incredibly honest and useful feedback and also support. Toward the end, there was a comment from one of his friends: "Rett, you are almost there. I'm so proud of you. I know this is your goal and you are going to make it! You are representing us all."

We had come so far from the days of fighting about his homework. It was incredible—but really, was it? I thought of a Jacob Riis quote I'd always kept on my desk when I taught:

> When nothing seems to help, I go and look at a stonecutter hammering away at his rock perhaps a hundred times without as much as a crack showing in it. Yet at the hundred and first blow it will split in two, and I know it was not that blow that did it, but all that had gone before.

That quote helped me to remember learning is a process, and there were many tough days when I needed the reminder. For some reason we don't think twice about having to say the word "mom" five hundred times before our child says it back to us, but when our kids get to high school we think we can teach something once and they should get it. Rett didn't get the self-directed cycle the first time it was introduced to him, or the second, or the third. In fact, for over three years he had been practicing it day in and day out and until this moment I wasn't sure he got it. The same was true for all of the other habits he was bringing to bear on this experience. There were moments during fifth and sixth grade when I wondered if he would ever be able to write a paragraph. But slowly, project by project, with continual and consistent practice and feedback, his skills had grown and developed over time. And now, in a context that was such a good fit for his interests and motivations, he was able to apply all of those skills and habits. The same would not have been true if he had been offered a chance to talk about soccer at an athletic coaches conference. He has no interest in soccer or high school athletics and it doesn't relate to his individual sense of purpose. He wouldn't have succeeded in that assignment, and he would have shown up as a very different kid if we had put him in such a position.

Rett's experience in Bulgaria was both successful and fulfilling. He worked incredibly hard, applied all he knew, leveraged all of his resources and supports, and by objective measures delivered a well-researched, well-written, compelling talk to an audience of over a hundred adults in a foreign country. There is no doubt he achieved something. The achievement was both made possible and fulfilling because it was aligned with his sense of purpose. Rett made so clear to me, we don't have to choose fulfillment or success for our kids. They can have both, and in fact, the best way to succeed is to seek fulfillment.

Rett's senior year will be upon us in a matter of months. Selfishly my heart already aches for the day he will pack his things and leave on his next adventure. I imagine his dog Nya and me sulking together on his bed, looking out the window and wishing he would come home. At the same time, I can't ignore my brewing excitement and anticipation for what his future holds. The knowledge he has of himself, the skills and habits he has built, and how they are all coming together in the sketches of his possible life paths are inspiring. I know how much he has to offer and in the quiet moments when he dares to dream, I do my best to make sure he knows as well. I'm not alone. His dad, his mentor, and a handful of others have begun to form a kitchen cabinet of sorts. As the people who know him, care about him, and pledged to support him, we've come together during this critical transition. Together we'll lend our experience and insights to make sure he is being true to himself and takes the concrete next step that fits him best. In no time at all, I will be walking the graduation processional, this time as a mom who knows her son is prepared.

Epilogue

For the third day in a row, Oscar's mom called. "He's still in his room. He's locked the door. He refuses to come out and won't go to school."

I sighed deeply, and after a long pause, said, "I'll be there in ten minutes." I grabbed my keys and purse, and on the way out, I stopped at the maintenance closet and grabbed a screwdriver.

The front door to Oscar's house was open. His mom sat on the edge of the couch with her head held in her hands. I took a seat across from her, and as she looked up at me I could see she'd been crying. Her eyes were red-rimmed and swollen. Her look said she was not only at her wit's end, totally frustrated by her son, but also scared.

I had so many questions. Didn't he have to eat? Use the

bathroom? Did she have a key? How was it possible for a fifteen-year-old boy to lock himself in his room for three days? But as I looked into Oscar's mom's face, I pushed them aside. *Not productive,* I thought. *She's doing everything she can in this moment.*

The feeling was recognizable to me. Over the first few years of Summit, Adam, Kelly, and I had experienced something similar—as had all of our colleagues at Summit. When working with teenagers, really working with them to develop and grow as human beings, there are points when it feels impossible. In some moments, you just run out of ideas or patience. In those instances, we realized it was time to "sub out." We needed to call someone else in who was fresh and able to look at things differently.

"Where's Oscar's room?" I asked.

She pointed to a door just to the right. I pulled my screwdriver from my bag and stood in front of it. She looked startled. "What are you going to do?"

I answered loudly, wanting Oscar to hear. "I'm going to take the hinges off the door. Oscar needs to be in school. I know he feels stuck and behind. We can work through that with him, but not if he's locked in his room."

His mom looked shocked. "Do you really think that will work?"

"Yes, it will work!" I said with too much exasperation. "There are ways to open locked doors, and taking the hinges off will absolutely work. I'm not leaving here without him."

Just then, the bedroom door cracked open and I found myself face-to-face with Oscar. His expression was filled with curiosity and surprise as he peered at me. I gave him a firm look and said, "You have five minutes to get dressed." He slowly nodded. And then hustled to grab his clothes.

A few blocks before we got to school, Oscar broke the silence in the car. "Were you really going to take the hinges off the door?"

Without thinking, I said, "Whatever it took, Oscar. I was going to do whatever it took. I'm not giving up on you."

He stared at me for a minute then turned to look out the window. As we pulled into the parking lot he said, "I believe you."

Whatever It Takes. WIT. You'll find the words or acronym in notes from our meetings at Summit, and posted in the copy room. You'll hear them in conversations among teachers and with students. WIT is in the stories we tell ourselves and one another. WIT is far more than a phrase, it's our culture. It is a mindset that drives our decisions. It's how we approach our work and what has driven us year after year. And, like everything we've ever done at Summit, Whatever It Takes has evolved over time.

Whatever It Takes doesn't mean we do everything *for* the kids.

It doesn't mean we accept the way things are and just work longer and harder to try to overcome.

It doesn't mean when we get stuck we lower our standards or give up.

In order to truly live Whatever It Takes, we find a way. We believe there is always a way to open a locked door.

It didn't take long for the screwdriver story to make the rounds at school, and before I knew it, I had a new nickname, "The Tavennator." (Arnold Schwarzenegger was California's governor at the time.) It was mostly whispered, but Kelly loved to call me "The Tavennator" in big public settings. Giggling every time, she would shake her head and hold up her fist as if grasping a screwdriver. I would smile and laugh, and at the same time my stomach would churn a bit. I didn't want to be "The Tavennator," but I also wasn't afraid of the role.

Fortunately, I'm not alone. I've met fellow Tavennators all across the country. They are teachers, principals, parents, and even students who simply don't accept that the door is locked and so many kids are shut out from being prepared. They are just as determined to open the door as I am.

In the fall of 2015, we launched the Summit Learning Program as a way of sharing our curriculum, professional development, and training and technology for free with other public schools who wanted to move toward real-world, project-based learning, self-direction, and reflective mentoring. My friend Julie, who had looked at me with exasperation when she'd asked, "What am I supposed to do, Diane? I can't start a school like you," was at the front of my mind as we started with nineteen schools not unlike the one her child attended.

We worked with fellow, like-minded educators whom we'd gotten to know through visits and conferences. Even so, it was a challenging year. Change is hard in any school, and these schools were really different from Summit. We'd never had the opportunity before to partner with a traditional large urban high school, or a rural one-room schoolhouse, and tailor our approach to their own community needs and values. But everyone was willing to do Whatever It Took, and by the end of the year we had collectively learned an enormous amount and enabled real progress for all of our kids. We'd also caught the attention of over one hundred more schools who wanted to join us.

We couldn't say no, and so embarked on a second year of collaboration and learning. We had made a lot of progress, but there was still so much to figure out as we were now working with public schools spread across twenty-seven states and in even more diverse school environments. But something was working because by the next year, over three hundred schools wanted to be part of our collaboration. When we began, every teacher in the Summit Learning Program could fit in one of our schools in California for a summer professional development training. By 2017, over three thousand teachers from forty states met in gymnasiums in thirteen different cities across the country. I tried to get to as many cities and towns as I could. I wanted to visit their classrooms, meet the students and teachers, talk with the principals, and eat a meal with them.

What I discovered in city after city and town after town was inspiring. The people engaged in the Summit Learning Program want what is best for kids. They are thirsty for resources, materials, and training to help them create learning experiences and schools that are real-world, self-directed, reflective, and collaborative. Countless teachers have described how they know their students and are doing the best teaching they have ever done. And in fact, a number of teachers have postponed planned retirements to continue teaching in the Summit Learning Program. They all say, "It's a lot of work, but it's worth it."

I've had dinner—and in a few cases lunch and breakfast—with these folks and many others in cities all across America, including Boston, Houston, L.A., New Orleans, Seattle, Chicago, Orlando, Detroit, New York, D.C., Denver, and San Francisco. I've also come together with people over some pretty amazing meals in small towns in Arkansas, Kansas, Missouri, Oklahoma, Utah, New Mexico, and many more states. There is nothing like food to bring people together. In every case, I've asked people to describe what learning looks like when we are truly preparing all kids for a fulfilled life.

Without exception, the vision is consistent: Kids are engaged. They're interested. They're doing real work, solving real problems. They work together. They get to know themselves and one another. They are driven by curiosity. Teachers coach, guide, mentor, and facilitate learning in a way that is inspiring, empowering, and sustainable. Of course kids learn to read and do math, but that's just the beginning. The students see value in the learning and the adults approach the process in a way that works for kids. So much more happens because learning isn't confined to six hours a day within the walls of a school building. It happens 24/7 across family, community, and school. Because we all want the same thing. We all want our kids to grow up to be self-sufficient, happy, contributing members of our society. And so we all play a role in their preparation.

I've sat with people from all races, genders, and political parties. Some people arrived on private jets and others took the city bus. Some people have run large unions, universities, and companies. Others have only ever worked for someone else. There are moms, dads, grandmothers, aunts, sisters, brothers. And two things have been consistently true across them all: everyone has a story of how they got to where they are; and they all can imagine something better for the kids they love.

Which makes me wonder how it's possible that in 2018 the headline for Gallup's annual report on American perceptions of education read, "Seven in 10 Parents Satisfied with Their Child's Education."[1] Had I only been talking to the 30 percent who weren't happy? Was it possible that 70 percent of parents were truly satisfied? Unlikely, because according to the same study, only 43 percent of Americans were satisfied with overall K–12 education quality in the U.S. We somehow separate—at least in our reporting—our individual experience from our impression of education as a whole. I believe the underlying narrative is that we've settled. But why? Why would anyone settle when it comes to their child and his future? And then I remember Oscar's mom, and the look on her face. She just didn't see another way. She felt alone, out of options, and didn't know what to do. Days later she would confide that she figured at some point he would have to come out, eventually things would get back to normal, and he would be fine.

"Fine" is the word I hear most often when talking with parents about their kids' education. "She'll be fine." "He'll be fine." It's a statement made usually after the parent has articulated a concern or pointed to a problem, something that just isn't right. In some cases the worries are extreme (drug use, bullying, depression, failing) and in others seemingly minor (boredom, stress, small academic setbacks). "She'll be fine" is generally coupled with the statement "This is life and kids need to learn how to deal with it. I had challenges. I made it through. I turned out fine."

What would happen if we expected more than fine? What would happen if being satisfied didn't mean your child was fine, but meant your child was great, and happy? I'm not talking about the shallow happiness young kids get from a piece of candy or a toy they really want. What if great meant they were fulfilled? What if they were engaged in purposeful work, community, and meaningful relationships?

At the dinners across the country, after we collectively paint a vision for what learning can and should look like, I ask the magic wand question: "We've waved our magic wand and the vision we've just painted for what learning can look like is real for *all* kids. We've succeeded! What does our country look like? What does our world look like?"

It usually takes a moment to get the conversation going. People need time to think. Sometimes the first person is tentative, and it takes a few more folks to weigh in before we get to a description of what the world would be like if every single child learned in the ways outlined in this book, if every child entered adulthood prepared for a fulfilled life.

"It's the world I want to live in."

"There wouldn't be poverty. People wouldn't go hungry and homeless."

"We'd be working together to solve the biggest challenges facing our country and our planet."

"People would feel empowered and able to take charge of their lives and engage in their communities and know they could make a difference."

"We'd be able to talk and work with people who are different from us and who hold different views. People would be accepted for who they are and valued for the uniqueness they bring."

"People would be happy and like what they're doing. They would have meaningful work and enough money to be free of stress."

The conversation generally picks up momentum and usually comes to a crescendo when someone says something really bold like "There would be no more war," or "We'd never lose another child in a school shooting."

The room goes quiet for a moment and people soak in the hope and optimism. And inevitably, the realism starts to seep in. Who do we think we are, sitting around a table and imagining we can bring peace? I'll admit, even I can get a bit intimidated when it's put in those terms. But I quickly realize where the conversation began. It started with kids. It started with real-world, self-directed, reflective, and collaborative learning. It started with adults believing they could prepare all kids to do more than basic reading and writing. It started with us embracing our foundational promise that all people have a right to life, liberty, and the pursuit of happiness. The pursuit of happiness, the good life, a fulfilled life. Right now the door to a fulfilled life is locked for far too many people. I say we take a screwdriver to the hinges.

What Now:
A Jump-Start to Bringing
Prepared Home

knew something was up. Usually when Mira and I travel together, we part ways as we enter the plane. We travel a lot, and both of us look forward to the hours on the plane to catch up on work or sometimes even a few hours of sleep before we hit the ground and begin running again. But today, Mira had specifically arranged for us to sit next to each other, and I could tell she was ready to talk. Mira joined Summit eight years ago, and for the last several years we've worked closely with parents across the country as the Summit Learning Program has grown.

We are both moms, but our kids are at very different stages. Her boys are one and five. She's thinking about her eldest starting kindergarten, and I'm helping Rett with college visits. We just don't seem to have that much in common right now, and so we aren't often talking parenting. But today was different. Mira needed to talk. She started before we even took off. The parenting expectations, Mira told me, seemed to change overnight. The noise of conflicting advice was getting louder; it felt like all the rules had changed, but no one had given her a road map to raising a happy and successful human being. She didn't have her son in weekday or weekend activities: Should he be in soccer and swimming or trying a martial arts class? How about art? Maybe that was something that would spark an early interest and curiosity.

While she and her husband made sure to read to their kids every night, her son didn't know his alphabet and certainly wasn't reciting the letters with the near perfection she saw in his classmates or some of her friends' kids. He could count to ten but seemed confused once he got past the number thirteen. There were the "preschool" enrichment books she could introduce, but she didn't have the energy to force him to sit down and focus, especially when they had such limited time together between school, jobs, travel, and her younger son. He was a sensitive, shy boy but also had, what felt like to Mira, an extra dose of energy, and he had a hard time focusing. How would he do in kindergarten? Would the teachers get to know him, and if they did, would they really *get* him?

Conversations, phone calls, and text messages with close friends and family members (many of whom were teachers or former teachers) certainly provided comfort. But Mira confided that she wasn't fully transparent with them about everything that worried her. While not always intentional, there is judgment in parenting and it is deeply personal.

Mira had dutifully studied and understood Summit's 16 Habits of Success (it was a part of her job, after all) and they all swam in her mind. Following all the best research, to be successful, she surmised that her boys ultimately needed to be calm and balanced in stressful situations, they needed to be able to direct and maintain their focus and emotions, understand their impact on others, build strong relationships, stay organized, have confidence in themselves, feel a sense of belonging, know what they were learning and its relevance to their lives, bounce back from challenges, make their own decisions, set goals, and be curious. And that was just the habits. How about the universal skills like being good problem-solvers? Her shoulders dropped in resignation as she recited the long list.

Who was responsible for teaching them all of this? When should she start? How should she start? What should she be doing at home, and what was fair to expect of her kids' schools, if anything?

She'd been talking non-stop for over an hour. I listened intently, remembering the pangs of guilt and worry I had felt as I wrestled with the very same questions about Rett. She drew in a deep breath, and with a big exhale said, "At the end of the day, I just want them to be happy. To be good human beings. To be surrounded by people who are different, who they could learn from. To know who they are, what they care about, and have the skills and opportunity to chase after it. And, if Summit has taught me anything, I don't want this at the expense of another kid or family. But it seems like those two things are in conflict."

"And, here I am," she observed. "I've got a good education, financial security, a comfortable home, and I know a lot about education. You are my captive audience for an entire flight, and I still have no idea what I can do right now for my boys. If I feel this way, how must most parents feel?"

It felt like I was having the Julie conversation all over again. This was not different from what we were hearing from parents in very diverse communities across the country. There was a common thread to their worry about their kids: "preparedness." How do I know if my child is prepared for life? What does it look like? And, what should *I* be doing?

The advice that's easy to give, yet hard to do, is this: **Be an advocate**. Chris Buja and the network of parents that formed the Community High School Foundation looked around and wanted better options for their kids, and for their community, and they banded together to demand it. The seismic shift in ideas about what kids really need starts with advocacy, and advocacy begins one conversation at a time.

We both looked at each other and knew just how unsatisfying this answer was. Mira is an advocate for kids all across the country, and she will be a strong one for her own children, but she also wanted something more immediate. She wanted support and reassurance. She wanted a brain trust to advise her, because she didn't have enough time to read all the latest parenting books. Most of her advice about parenting came from her friends who also had young children, but this, too, can be fraught.

As the hours passed, we did what we always do; we started to ask why. Why did Mira want this? Why did she feel so alone? Why were all of the supports she had leaving her feeling unprepared to be the parent she wants to be? By the time we stepped off that flight, we had committed to finding a way to support *all* parents. We know it's one thing to read a book but something entirely different to bring this book to life for you and your family.

This was the beginning of preparedforsuccess.org, a website devoted to supporting parents who want to ready their children for the world they will graduate into. Parents can use it to bring real-world learning into their everyday life and to help their children at any age develop the skills of self-direction, collaboration, and reflection. It's a resource for parents who don't want to be tiger moms, or helicopter, snowplow, and/or free-range parents. It's a community of parents who want to prepare their kids to be happy and to live fulfilled lives. Raising kids is a journey, and we hope that preparedforsuccess.org can help you navigate it.

We've taken the same approach we took with Summit. We've started with rigorous scientific research, but as working moms, we've married it with the practical limitations facing most parents. Also like Summit, it's a model we need to be patient with, one we need to be willing to let evolve as we get better and better information. For those reasons, our website is the best place to seek up-to-date ideas and concrete suggestions.

As of the writing of this book, though, we've compiled a set of activities you can start using in your home and life with your family. These are compiled from throughout *Prepared* so it's easy for you to look through the accompanying chapter for more information.

REAL-WORLD AND PROJECT-BASED LEARNING

Seek out opportunities to engage your child's opinion and participation

Many parents feel it's their job to oversee and correct homework, but their role in their child's learning can go so much further. Kids can take on projects like mapping out transportation options to school, helping figure out a plan to deal with the weird noise the car is making, or researching which cleaning products are the most healthy and safe to use around kids and pets. We don't usually engage kids in these kinds of activities, in part because it's faster and easier not to, and in part because we think they don't care. But remember what my student James told me when he was practicing his speech on farm subsidies: "Just because we're young doesn't mean we don't care about things."

SELF-DIRECTION

Make the self-directed cycle part of your everyday life

Even if your child's school does not teach a self-directed cycle, there's no reason you can't teach it and support it at home: They can set a goal, make a plan, carry out the plan, show what they know, and reflect. This cycle can be used for anything a child wants to pursue, from cooking dinner one night a week to making a case for the activity your family will do next weekend.

Teach the five power behaviors of a self-directed learner

The cycle is a great guide, as are the behaviors that power it:

1. Strategy-shifting
2. Challenge-seeking
3. Persistence
4. Responding to setbacks
5. Appropriate help-seeking

These are ideas you likely parent to anyway, but having a common language and framework to put them in can be helpful. You can call these behaviors out when you see them in your child, and ask your child to point them out in others.

Emphasize effective goal-setting

The earlier you start this with your children the better. Every child is capable of setting goals and it's a process that is invaluable to them as they grow into school and adulthood. Introduce your child to SMART goals: Goals that are Specific, Measurable, Actionable, Realistic, and Timebound.

The goals they set should matter to them so that their motivation is internal, not external. They can think big and set large, aspirational goals (and practice how to achieve them), but they should also set smaller, simpler goals—particularly when they're younger. Help them by talking through their plan to reach those goals, what potential obstacles might arise, and how they might get past those obstacles. Check in with them regularly to offer help.

Model effective goal-setting yourself, too. When you set a goal, verbalize why it meets a SMART goal criteria. Then ask them to do the same.

Remember that skill development is lumpy

Don't get discouraged. Failure is part of the deal. Remember the quote of the stonecutter—sometimes it takes a long time before you can see the impact of your efforts.

> When nothing seems to help, I go and look at a stonecutter hammering away at his rock perhaps a hundred times without as much as a crack showing in it. Yet at the hundred and first blow it will split in two, and I know it was not that blow that did it, but all that had gone before.

Catch yourself when you need to be needed by your child

Let the discomfort wash over you. This slow letting go is part of the greater process of preparing your child. Be willing to be needed differently.

REFLECTION THROUGH MENTORING

Mentor; don't direct

Just as I had to learn not to step in and take over when Rett began cooking, take a step back. Give feedback and guidance without giving answers. Ask questions that help your child reflect on what they want, who they are, what they care about, how they feel, and, ultimately, what they should do as a result. This isn't about you telling them what to do but about them making authentic choices for themselves.

Focus on the "ings"

Instead of asking, "What do you want to be?", ask questions that get to underlying interests. Ask questions like: "What do you like doing?" "What parts of that do you like most?" Help your child figure out that they like creat**ing**, or talk**ing**, perform**ing**, or problem-solv**ing**; "ings" that will go far toward helping them better know themselves.

Asking the right questions

When your child inevitably has an interpersonal conflict, see it as an opportunity to teach the skills needed to mediate conflict, repair relationships, collaborate, and reflect. There are a set of questions Summit mentors use all the time that are also helpful when parenting. They are open-ended questions that most often lead to thoughtful answers. You can ask:

- What do you want from this situation?
- What emotions do you have?
- What behaviors are you exhibiting?
- What is working or not working? Why?
- Put yourself in the other person's shoes: What do you think their perspective is?
- What role can you play in getting to your desired outcome?
- Is there anything you need to do to make the relationship right?

This can be done in conversation with your child, or in written form if that is preferred. Growth occurs with support and guidance, whether that's from a parent, mentor, or teacher.

COLLABORATION

Teach the principles of consensus

Two incredibly helpful tools we've used at Summit are the decision grid and STP.

With the decision grid, you can explain that your goal is to reach consensus but that certain decisions will ultimately land with you, or will be yours to veto. (Refer to the sample grid on page 259.) This grid has enormous potential in a household, as families navigate everything from what movie to watch to what a reasonable curfew is. With STP, when your family reaches an impasse, practice first turning the problem into a question. Then, identify the status by clearly communicating with each other, without judgment, why each person feels the way they do. Define the target—the marks that will be checked off if you've reached a resolution. Finally, if the decision grid allows, develop proposals to get there.

SaMPLe DeCiSiOn GrId

This grid can be useful for documenting who is in each role for a set of decisions.

	Stakeholder #1	Stakeholder #2	Stakeholder #3	Stakeholder #4
Decision A	Role	Role	Role	Role
Decision B	Role	Role	Role	Role

Role Codes

D / Decision: Person or people who make the decision

P / Proposal: Person or people who are involved in developing the proposal

I / Input: Person or people who provide input on the proposal

V / Veto: Person or people who can veto the decision

MBI / Must Be Informed: Person or people who must be informed of the decision

---

SUCCESSFUL HABITS

Ask why, then ask why again

If you are in conflict with your child about anything from bedtime to homework, approach the conflict with curiosity. In my case, I employed this style of questioning with Rett when, to my mind, he never did his homework, and I ended up learning a lot not only about the way his brain works but also about what he was really being asked to do. Ask why of yourself, too. Why is it so important to you that something happen in a certain way? So often we go along with rules "just because" but when you ask why, they often don't make a lot of sense. This might be an opportunity for advocacy.

CURIOSITY-DRIVEN KNOWLEDGE

Use Expose, Explore, and Pursue as a tool for enrichment activities

Summit's Adam Carter created the Expose, Explore, and Pursue framework and tested it with researchers who focus on building purpose. It can be used at school and at home, and it provides the best guide that I know of to help you choose how to spend your time with your kids and family, including after-school and weekend activities.

As I learned when seeking a dojo for Rett, not all activities are created equal. Recognizing that there are budget and logistical limitations, exposing your child to new places and experiences will connect them in deeper ways to the broader world around them, and that will teach them skills that translate to their time outside of the activity. Not every activity will stick, and that is okay. But if something sparks their curiosity, help your child to explore it more deeply and try it beyond that first experience. And, if the spark turns into an interest, open the doors to help them pursue it further.

Also avoid a packed schedule. Downtime is time to be exposed to new interests and to explore and pursue those interests. Remember Brody and his passion for roller coasters. It's tempting for parents to urge "productive" activities, when really exploring interests helps your child understand himself and his sense of purpose.

Engage in knowledge acquisition together

Don't dismiss technology in one fell swoop but rather explore on the internet together. Spend time making connections between *why* something might be important to know. It's too easy to say, "Just buckle down and learn this." Instead, help them see why it matters.

A CONCRETE NEXT STEP

Reframe the college search

When looking at colleges, encourage your child to look at schools not for their football team or familiarity but to ask if the school is:

- Consistent with a vision they have created for their life as an adult based upon the knowledge they have of themselves
- Purposeful and realistic
- A fully informed choice from a set of real options
- Supported by family and community

Encourage Plan B thinking

Even if they get into their first-choice school and pursue what they most want, thinking through and exploring other options will help them have a more flexible approach to their future; one that's more grounded in who they are than what rigid path might be available at the moment.

We hope the activities, tools, and resources on prepared forsuccess.org become a trusted resource that helps you to cut through the noise to make navigating parenting, learning, and school easier. Mira and I want to be part of a community of parents who support one another to be confident in our decisions and in the choices we are making for our kids.

Join us in being *Prepared* parents.

Acknowledgments

The stories and ideas in *Prepared* belong to a community of people who have engaged with one another on behalf of all kids for the better part of two decades. I am humbled to have the opportunity to share my perspective of their story in *Prepared*. The gratitude I have is immense and will inevitably be woefully underrepresented here.

In January 2018, Todd Rose spent a week of his vacation teaching me how to write a book, and I can't imagine a more gifted teacher. *Prepared* is a direct result of his mentorship, encouragement, support, generosity, and friendship. So many of the ideas in *Prepared* are influenced by the important work he is doing at Populace with his cofounder Parisa Rouhani, whose personal story inspires me and whose incisive insights make me better. Together they are truly seeking a better world for us all.

One of Todd's numerous gifts was an introduction to my incredible agent, Howard Yoon. During one of our first calls, Howard gave me an assignment—write the hardest story you have to write. With a perfect combination of care and expectation, he said, "I want you to write until it is hard but not painful." He has more than fulfilled his promise to be there for me every step of the way. One of Howard's most admirable skills is his ability to bring people together.

Introducing me to Tina Constable at Crown Currency was a profoundly important step. From the very first moment, Tina not only understood but embraced the vision for *Prepared*. As a mother and female professional, Tina has been an unwavering champion and advocate for the book and its ideas. I admire her creative vision and am grateful for her leadership.

Fortunately for me, Tina and Roger Scholl are a team. I knew I would be fortunate to have Roger as my editor, for his combination of expertise and compassion made him a steady and supportive guide through a process which could have been confusing for a novice like me. I held my breath each time I shared another part of *Prepared* with Roger, only to be rewarded with insightful feedback that helped me learn and helped *Prepared* be better. Erin Little was a constant presence for us all, and she helped us stay on track during a relatively rapid schedule.

But before meeting the talented and dedicated Currency team, there was Jenna Free. I needed a collaborator, and Howard thought he might know the perfect person. I will never forget our first call; within minutes I knew I wanted to work with Jenna, and I couldn't stop myself from saying so. It was a fortuitous instinct that has proven to be one of the most rewarding of my life. Jenna is so many things—an incredibly talented writer, a skilled project manager, a brilliant editor, a totally flexible collaborator, and a curious learner. On early morning calls, during late-night editing sessions, and throughout so many weekends, Jenna coaxed *Prepared* into existence, and along the way I discovered she *is* a prepared parent and a committed and loyal friend.

It is an embarrassment of riches to have one strong, brilliant, passionate female partner, and somehow I got lucky enough to have two. For the last eight years, Mira Browne has been my partner and indefatigable champion for all kids. Mira is one of the most persistent and hardest-working people I know. Her willingness to bring her insights, experiences, and expertise to *Prepared* has shaped the pages and, perhaps more important, the opportunity to support parents going forward. The magical and idyllic writing retreat with Jenna and Mira will most certainly be a part of the highlight reel of my life.

Mira is one of so many members of the Summit community who gave selflessly during the creation of *Prepared*. Jimmy Zuniga, Zack Miller, Jon Deane, Lizzie Choi, Malia Burns, Nathan James, Yelenna Arzu, and a brilliant and inspiring group of Summit prep students shared stories and insights that fill the book. But, of course, more important, they do the work day in and day out that makes Summit what it is. I have tremendous respect for these generous folks.

Kelly Garcia and Adam Carter not only allowed but encouraged me to tell our story. The hours we spent remembering and reminiscing were joyful and productive, and I am grateful for their willingness to read and comment along the way. For the past sixteen years, I have had the honor and pleasure of doing work we all deeply believe in side by side with these two spectacular educators and parents. What a gift they both are to me personally and to our profession.

The three of us may have never met if not for the vision, commitment, and tenacity of the founding families of Summit. I am eternally grateful to Chris Buja for placing that first ad and his twenty years of service, and for the hundreds of families who joined him, giving of their time, talent, and treasure to breathe life into the idea of Summit. Summit exists today because a community came together in a quest to create something for their own children, for other people's children, and for our world.

"Build it and they will come" doesn't always work out. If not for the first class of Summit students and families, we wouldn't have a story to tell. For me, there will never be another school community that more embodies all six of our core values—courage, compassion, curiosity, integrity, respect, and responsibility. I can only hope *Prepared* honors the contribution and love of this very special group of people.

So often, as a community grows and ages, it loses its way. For twenty years, a small, dedicated group, serving as Summit's board of directors, have guarded Summit's vision and mission. Paul Koontz, John Novitsky, Stacey Keare, Beth Bartlett, Bob O'Donnell, Steve Humphreys, Blake Warner, Andrew Thompson, Diego Arambula, and Meg Whitman all deserve my immense gratitude. If not for their experience, insight, courage, commitment, and support through both challenge and success, I am convinced Summit would not exist. For the last eleven years, Bob Oster has masterfully led their efforts. I can't imagine there is a better board chair in the world. It would be impossible to detail all of his invaluable wisdom, but it is easy to remember his focus. In all the years I have known him, we've never had a conversation without him asking, "What is best for the kids?"

For most of my life, my personal story was something I ran from. It seemed easiest to bury the past under achievement and hard work, but I didn't realize I was burying myself along the way.

I am deeply grateful to Kim Smith for having the vision and talent to create a perfect opportunity for me to begin discovering myself in the Pahara Institute, and for seeing in me what I couldn't see in myself. Under Kim's skilled guidance in partnership with Tia Martinez and John Simpkins, I first found a community and ultimately a family that showed me what it means to love unconditionally. With the support of Aimee, Aylon, Brian, Christina, David, Emily, Greg, Jay, Jim, Joe, Joel, Karen, Kim, Kriste, MJ, Mike, Stacey, Susan, Tom, Trish, and Vanessa, I first learned to tell my story. I am so honored and grateful to be a part of our family.

Joyce, MaryAnn, Robin, Valerie, and I were English teachers from different school districts charged with creating a writing assessment. Writing brought us together, but books kept us together. Over twenty years and hundreds of books later, we are no longer a book club but a family. So much of what I know of how to be a mother, partner, teacher, leader, and friend has come from the incredible modeling and authentic sharing of these beautiful and admirable women. Their love, encouragement, and nurturing have shaped who I am today.

A few years ago, my sister and our families were gathered around the dinner table telling stories when my youngest niece looked at us and said, "I know you guys were poor, and life was really hard when you were growing up, but it seems like you still had fun with each other." I've always believed that if you are looking for truth, ask a child. To this day, the deepest and most authentic laughs I've ever had have been with my sister, Dee. Pure joy is one of the many gifts she shares so unselfishly, as is the most precious gift of her beautiful family—Brittany, Jake, Brooke, and Trent.

It seems fitting that the last paragraph I write for this book is for Scott and Rett. For in so many ways, they are the book. *Prepared* is our story, the story of our journey to discover who we are as individuals and as a family. *Prepared* exists because Scott and Rett encouraged and enabled me to do the work I love, even when it took me away from them. It exists because when I thought I couldn't go on anymore, Rett looked at me and said, "Mom, other kids need you more than I do right now—go." I don't know the words to express the depth of my gratitude and love for them. I can only hope they feel it when I embrace them.

Notes

CHAPTER 1

1. Jennifer E. Lansford, PhD, et al., "A Public Health Perspective on School Dropout and Adult Outcomes: A Prospective Study of Risk and Protective Factors from Age 5 to 27," *Journal of Adolescent Health* 58, no. 6 (June 2016): 652–58, https://doi.org/10.1016/j.jadohealth.2016.01.014.
2. D. A. Laird, and E. C. Laird, *Sizing Up People: How to judge and analyze personality, intelligence, and abilities in others for greater personal happiness and business success for yourself* (New York, NY: McGraw-Hill Education, 1964), 46.
3. Avil Beckford, "The Skills You Need to Succeed in 2020," *Forbes*, August 6, 2018, https://www.forbes.com/sites/ellevate/2018/08/06/the-skills-you-need-to-succeed-in-2020/#48e6d098288a.
4. Gwendolyn Mink and Alice O'Connor, eds., *Poverty in the United States: An Encyclopedia of History, Politics, and Policy*, vol. 1 (Santa Barbara, CA: ABC-CLIO, 2004), 41.

CHAPTER 4

1. Katherine Ellison and Louis Freedberg, "Project-Based Learning on the Rise Under the Common Core," *EdSource*, April 27, 2015,

https://edsource.org/2015/project-based-learning-on-the-rise-under-the-common-core/78851.

2. W. R. Penuel and B. Means, "Designing a Performance Assessment to Measure Students' Communication Skills in Multimedia-Supported Project-Based Learning (paper presented at the Annual Meeting of the American Educational Research Association, New Orleans, LA, 2000); also see William J. Stepien, Shelagh A. Gallagher, and David Workman, "Problem-Based Learning for Traditional and Interdisciplinary Classrooms," *Journal for the Education of the Gifted* 16, no. 4 (June 1, 1993): 338–57, https://doi.org/10.1177/016235329301600402.

3. W. Parker et al., "Rethinking Advanced High School Coursework: Tackling the Depth/Breadth Tension in the AP U.S. Government and Politics Course," *Journal of Curriculum Studies* 43, no. 4 (2011): 533–59, https://doi.org/10.1080/00220272.2011.584561.

4. U.S. Department of Education, Regional Educational Laboratory at WestEd, *Effects of Problem Based Economics on High School Economics Instruction*, by Neal Finkelstein et al., NCEE 2010-4002 (Washington, D.C., July 2010), https://ies.ed.gov/ncee/edlabs/regions/west/pdf/REL_20104012.pdf.

5. Gulbahar Beckett and Paul Chamness Miller, eds., *Project-Based Second and Foreign Language Education: Past, Present, and Future* (Greenwich, CT: Information Age Publishing, 2006); C. Horan, C. Lavaroni, and P. Beldon, *Observation of the Tinker Tech Program Students for Critical Thinking and Social Participation Behaviors* (Novato, CA: Buck Institute for Education, 1996); John Mergendoller, Nan Maxwell, and Yolanda Bellisimo, "The Effectiveness of Problem-Based Instruction: A Comparative Study of Instructional Methods and Student Characteristics," *Interdisciplinary Journal of Problem-Based Learning* 1, no. 2 (2006): 49–69, https://doi.org/10.7771/1541-5015.1026; R. Tretten and P. Zachariou, *Learning About Project-Based Learning: Assessment of Project-Based Learning in Tinkertech Schools* (San Rafael, CA: The Autodesk Foundation, 1995). John Thomas, *A Review of Research on Project-Based Learning* (report prepared for The Autodesk Foundation,

March 2000), retrieved from http://www.bobpearlman.org/BestPractices/PBL_Research.pdf; Andrew Walker and Heather Leary, "A Problem-Based Learning Meta Analysis: Differences Across Problem Types, Implementation Types, Disciplines, and Assessment Levels," *Interdisciplinary Journal of Problem-Based Learning* 3, no. 1 (2009): 12–43, https://doi.org/10.7771/1541-5015.1061.

6. Jo Boaler, "Learning from Teaching: Exploring the Relationship Between Reform Curriculum and Equity," *Journal for Research in Mathematics Education* 33, no. 4 (July 2002): 239–58; Penuel and Means, "Designing a Performance Assessment to Measure Students' Communication Skills."

7. West Virginia Department of Education, Division of Teaching and Learning, Office of Research, *Extended Professional Development in Project-Based Learning*, by Nate Hixson, Jason Ravitz, and Andy Whisman (Charleston, WV, September 2012), https://files.eric.ed.gov/fulltext/ED565466.pdf; Johannes Strobel and Angela van Barneveld, "When Is PBL More Effective? A Meta-synthesis of Meta-analyses Comparing PBL to Conventional Classrooms," *Interdisciplinary Journal of Problem-Based Learning* 3, no. 1 (March 2009): 44–58, https://doi.org/10.7771/1541-5015.1046.

8. PBL Works, "Research Brief: PBL Helps Students Become Better Decision Makers," Buck Institute for Education, accessed February 23, 2019, http://www.bie.org/blog/research_brief_pbl_helps_students_become_better_decision_makers; Xin Zhang, et al., "Improving Children's Competence as Decision Makers: Contrasting Effects of Collaborative Interaction and Direct Instruction," *American Educational Research Journal* 53, no. 1 (February 2016): 194–223, https://doi.org/10.3102/0002831215618663.

CHAPTER 5

1. Carol Dweck, *Mindset: The New Psychology of Success* (New York, NY: Random House, 2007).

CHAPTER 7

1. Erik Larson, "New Research: Diversity + Inclusion = Better Decision Making at Work," *Forbes,* September 21, 2017, https://www.forbes.com/sites/eriklarson/2017/09/21/new-research-diversity-inclusion-better-decision-making-at-work/#4eac27 ac4cbf.

CHAPTER 8

1. https://www.turnaroundusa.org/.

CHAPTER 9

1. David Duran, "Learning-by-Teaching. Evidence and Implications as a Pedagogical Mechanism," *Innovations in Education and Teaching International* 54, no. 5 (February 2016): 476–84, https://doi.org/10.1080/14703297.2016.1156011.
2. Donna Recht and Lauren Leslie, "Effect of Prior Knowledge on Good and Poor Readers' Memory of Text," *Journal of Educational Psychology* 80, no. 1 (March 1988): 16–20.

   Further resources with similar findings include: D. Schwartz, J. M. Tsang, and K.P. Blair, *The ABCs of How We Learn: 26 Scientifically Proven Approaches, How They Work and When to Use Them* (New York: W. W. Norton & Company, 2016); Peter Brown, Henry Roediger, and Mark McDaniel, *Make It Stick: The Science of Successful Learning* (Cambridge, MA: Belknap Press, 2014).
3. Sarah J. Priebe, Janice M. Keenan, and Amanda C. Miller, "How Prior Knowledge Affects Word Identification and Comprehension," *Reading and Writing* 25, no. 1 (January 2012): 131–49, https://link.springer.com/article/10.1007%2Fs11145-010-9260-0; John Bransford and Marcia Johnson, "Contextual Prerequisites for Understanding: Some Investigations of Comprehension and Recall," *Journal of Verbal Learning & Verbal Behavior* 11, no. 6 (December 1972): 717–26; Danielle McNamara and Walter Kintsch, "Learning from Texts: Effects of Prior Knowledge and Text Coherence," *Discourse Processes* 22, no. 3 (1996): 247–82; Katherine A. Rawson and James P. Van Overschelde, "How Does Knowledge Promote Memory? The Distinctiveness Theory of Skilled Memory," *Journal of Memory and Language* 58, no. 3 (2008):

646–68; Recht and Leslie, "Effect of Prior Knowledge on Good and Poor Readers' Memory of Text"; George Spilich et al., "Text Processing of Domain-Related Information for Individuals with High and Low Domain Knowledge," *Journal of Verbal Learning & Verbal Behavior* 18, no. 3 (June 1979): 275–90.

4. Anya Kamenetz, "Forget Screen Time Rules—Lean In to Parenting Your Wired Child, Author Says," NPR.org, January 15, 2019, https://www.npr.org/2019/01/15/679304393/forget-screen-time-rules-lean-in-to-parenting-your-wired-child.

5. American Academy of Pediatrics, "American Academy of Pediatrics Announces New Recommendations for Children's Media Use," October 21, 2016, https://www.aap.org/en-us/about-the-aap/aap-press-room/Pages/American-Academy-of-Pediatrics-Announces-New-Recommendations-for-Childrens-Media-Use.aspx.

CHAPTER 11

1. Benjamin L. Castleman, Lindsay C. Page, and Ashley L. Snowdon, "SDP Summer Melt Handbook: A Guide to Investigating and Responding to Summer Melt," Strategic Data Project, Center for Education Policy Research, Harvard University, 2013, https://sdp.cepr.harvard.edu/files/cepr-sdp/files/sdp-summer-melt-handbook.pdf.

2. Kate Stringer, "'Summer Melt': Why Are Hundreds of Thousands of Freshmen Dropping Out of College Before Day One?" *The 74*, September 5, 2016, https://www.the74million.org/article/summer-melt-why-are-hundreds-of-thousands-of-freshmen-dropping-out-of-college-before-day-one/.

3. National Center for Education Statistics, Digest of Education Statistics, "Table 326.20: Graduation Rate from First Institution Attended Within 150 Percent of Normal Time for First-Time, Full-Time Degree/Certificate-Seeking Students at 2-Year Postsecondary Institutions, by Race/Ethnicity, Sex, and Control of Institution: Selected Cohort Entry Years, 2000 Through 2014," accessed February 24, 2019, https://nces.ed.gov/programs/digest/d18/tables/dt18_326.20.asp.

4. Anthony P. Carnevale, Ban Cheah, and Andrew R. Hanson, "The

Economic Value of College Majors, Executive Summary," Georgetown University Center on Education and the Workforce, 2015, https://cew.georgetown.edu/wp-content/uploads/Exec-Summary-web-B.pdf, 5.

5. Sharon Noguchi, "Report: Only 30% of Ninth-Graders Will Graduate from College," *San Jose Mercury News*, November 27, 2017, https://www.mercurynews.com/2017/11/27/report-only-30-of-ninth-graders-will-graduate-from-college/.

6. National Center for Education Statistics, Digest of Education Statistics, "Average Total Tuition, Fees, Room and Board Rates Charged for Full-Time Undergraduate Students in Degree-Granting Institutions, by Level and Control of Institution: Selected Years, 1984–85 to 2015–16," accessed February 24, 2019, https://nces.ed.gov/fastfacts/display.asp?id=76.

7. Abigail Hess, "This Is the Age Most Americans Pay Off Their Student Loans," CNBC, July 3, 2017, https://www.cnbc.com/2017/07/03/this-is-the-age-most-americans-pay-off-their-student-loans.html.

EPILOGUE

1. Megan Brenan, "Seven in 10 Parents Satisfied with Their Child's Education," Gallup, August 27, 2018, https://news.gallup.com/poll/241652/seven-parents-satisfied-child-education.aspx.

Index

Reader's Guide

PART I

1. Diane's beliefs about education were shaped both by her childhood experiences and by her work as an educator. How have your life experiences shaped your beliefs? Do you see echoes of those experiences in the way you teach, lead, or parent?
2. What does leading a good life mean to you?
3. A significant piece of Summit's approach is that it questions educational conventions that tend to be taken for granted, like graduation ceremonies or what the role of the teacher looks like. Which conventions do you think you've taken for granted and why?
4. Diane writes about "the nuclear arms race for college admissions." What is the impact of that arms race on your child or your students?
5. What do you believe should be the tried-and-true formula for getting into college? What trade-offs, if any, are we making if we can prepare all kids for both college and a good life? How is what you want out of life different from what your parents' generation wanted?
6. How is what your children or students want different from what you want?
7. What skills do you think are most important for an adult to have today? How do those vary between work and home?
8. Describe the culture of competition in your preschool/elementary school/high school. Is it overt or subtle? In what ways do you think it influences behavior?

9. In what ways does a community have power to influence education? In what ways has your community shaped the education opportunities that surround you?
10. If you set out to create your ideal school from scratch, what would it look like?

PART II

1. What real-world learning opportunities did you have as a student? What do you remember about them? Were they effective or ineffective, and what made them so?
2. Without attaching judgment, what might have been different in your life if your education had been more engaging?
3. School quality is primarily determined by standardized test scores. Do you think this is appropriate? What incentives does this approach provide to educators and parents?
4. What are ways to bring real-world, project-based learning into a child's life, outside of school? Are there extracurricular activities or family activities that lend themselves to lasting learning experiences? What questions do you consider when selecting these activities?
5. Many people believe that self-direction is inherent, and not something one can learn. Do you agree or disagree, and why?
6. Do you think it's possible to be a fulfilled adult without being self-directed? Why or why not?
7. Do you already use a form of the self-directed cycle in the course of your day? Where do you use it, and what does it look like?
8. What is your relationship with failure, and how—if at all— does that translate to how you view it for your child or students? What experiences could you create for your kids and/or students to experience failure and learn from it, similar to Diane's cooking story with her son?
9. Most people have established roles with their kids or students. What is your established role? What fears do you have about it changing?
10. What impact did mentors play in your life?
11. What do you see as the differences between teacher, parent, and mentor? Where do the roles intersect?

12. In what ways is grading useful to the process of learning, and in what ways is it ineffective, or even harmful?

13. What do you want to know about how your child is doing in school? Is that reflective in your child's grades? If not, how do you get that information?

14. What are some of your "ings" (interests that are unique to you), and how did you come to understand what they were?

15. What do you see as school's role in helping students understand their professional interests?

16. What are some ways we might stifle the role of competition in school? Would you see this as a plus or a minus, and why?

17. Are most group decisions in your life made by consensus or majority rule? What do you see as the benefits and drawbacks of each?

18. To what extent do you think group work is valued in the workplace today?

19. Are real-world projects, self-direction, reflection, and collaboration approaches you could implement at your school? What are the obstacles?

PART III

1. What building blocks do you emphasize in your parenting or teaching? Which building blocks do you think you've neglected?

2. Did you resonate with Kelly's or Diane's position with regard to Zack? Or both? Were they far off from each other, and what would you have done in that moment?

3. What habits do you feel are most important to teach your kids or students, and how are you teaching them?

4. What's the role of homework in your family or classroom? Is it effective?

5. What do you see as the role of knowledge in the future? Is it something we will still need?

6. Why do you think it might be hard for teachers to adopt a different role in the classroom?

7. What do you think defines a good teacher? Where do your beliefs come from?

8. What are some ways you can promote Expose, Explore, and Pursue in your child's life or in your students' lives? What role can the community play in this?

9. How important do you think it is for kids to follow their curiosities and interests?

10. How do you feel about the Internet's role in helping kids delve into interests?

11. At Innovation Summit, Frederick suggests that it's unethical to let fear of a failed technique block progress; the stakes are too high to do nothing when you can do something. Do you agree or disagree? How do you think a fear of failure has held back different industries and innovations, if at all?

12. To what extent do you feel it's important for kids to name and understand their developing skills?

13. Do you think planning out multiple pathways is helpful? Have you done this in your life?

14. Why do you think it's important to have a concrete next step? Did you have one, and if not, why?

15. What types of networks of support helped you with your education and career path? How can we connect more young people to similar "kitchen cabinets"?

16. Why might people feel that preparing for college is at odds with preparing for life?

EPILOGUE

1. Diane explains that one of the most frequent comments she hears from parents, when thinking of their own schooling, is "I did fine." Is this a reasonable, pragmatic answer? Or is it settling? What is fair to expect?

2. If you had the opportunity to wave your magic wand, and we achieved this approach to learning for all kids, what does our country look like? What does our world look like?

Diane Tavenner is pioneering a new vision for education in the United States. As the cofounder and CEO of Summit Public Schools, a nationally recognized nonprofit that operates fifteen public middle and high schools in California and Washington, Diane developed a school model centered on real-world experiences, self-direction, collaboration, and reflection—preparing all students to succeed in college, thrive in today's workplace, and lead a secure and fulfilled life. All net proceeds from the sale of this book will be donated to a student scholarship fund.

A lifelong educator, Diane spent a decade as a public school teacher, administrator, and leader in traditional urban and suburban public schools throughout California. She founded Summit Preparatory Charter High School in 2003, which quickly earned a reputation as one of the nation's best public high schools, and she ultimately grew one successful school into a network of public middle and high schools across two states.

In 2015, Summit launched the Summit Learning Program to offer curriculum, professional development, and ongoing support to schools across the country. Today, the program is partnering with thousands of educators and hundreds of schools in diverse communities across the country.

Summit has earned many accolades and distinctions, most notably America's Best High Schools from *U.S. News & World Report*, America's Most Challenging High Schools by *The Wash-*

ington Post, and one of the world's Top 10 Most Innovative Companies in Education from *Fast Company*. To date, 99 percent of Summit graduates have been accepted into four-year colleges, and its graduates complete college at double the national average. Summit is also recognized for its commitment to continuous improvement and collaboration, establishing innovative partnerships across industries, including with renowned learning scientists and researchers, universities, technology companies, teacher preparation programs, foundations, and community organizations.

Diane serves on the board of T.L.P. Education, Transcend, and the Carnegie Foundation for the Advancement of Teaching and Learning. She was previously the board chair of the California Charter Schools Association, representing the vast majority of California's charter schools. Diane is a member and moderator of the Pahara-Aspen Education Fellowship, a fellow in the Broad Academy, and a chapter chairperson and member of the Young Presidents Organization.

Diane is a frequent speaker at the nation's top entrepreneurship and education conferences, including ASU+GSV, the Foundation for Excellence in Education, and SXSWedu with Bill Gates.

Diane holds a bachelor's degree in psychology and sociology from the University of Southern California and has a master's degree in administration and policy analysis from Stanford University.